# THE GREAT
# BLACK SWAMP II:

### *MORE historical tales of*
### *northwestern ohio*

D1596532

*photography & narrative by*

# JIM MOLLENKOPF

# THE GREAT BLACK SWAMP II

*MORE historical tales of northwestern ohio*

*photography & narrative by*

## JIM MOLLENKOPF

©2000 Lake of the Cat Publishing,
P.O. Box 351454, Toledo, Ohio, 43635-1454
*ISBN 0-9665910-2-X*
*Library of Congress Control 00-090673*

# Table of Contents:

# List of Illustrations And Photographs

2

*MORE HISTORICAL TALES OF NORTHWESTERN OHIO*

# Foreword

The year 1790 found northwest Ohio in nearly the same state as it had been for untold centuries. In the east, a young United States of America was feeling its oats, having defeated the reigning superpower of the world a few years earlier in the American Revolution. To the south, settlers and Indians were clashing along the Ohio River, and in the states and territories that bordered it. And to the north, a fledgling frontier settlement was taking root in Detroit. But northwest Ohio remained almost pristine, and its native population lived their lives virtually undisturbed.

But hurricane winds of change were building on the horizon. In the next few years the United States would send three armies to the Ohio frontier to do battle with the Indians before finally winning at Fallen Timbers. After Fallen Timbers, the Great Black Swamp lay in the way, but not for long. The sheer enormity of the will and energy of tens of thousands of land-hungry settlers soon overpowered it. Fifty years later in 1840, the land in northwest Ohio had undergone considerable change and its aboriginal population had been almost completely replaced by a European one.

A judge who had traveled through the Maumee Valley and northwest Ohio in the late 1790's and early 1800's and had enjoyed the hospitality of various Indian tribes traveled through it again around that time. He wrote, "not an indication remained of the very extensive Indian villages which I had formerly seen there. It seemed almost impossible that in so short a period such an astonishing change could have taken place."

Here are some of the stories about that change as well as of other characters and events of the late 18th to mid 19th centuries in northwest Ohio. The book is a follow-up to *The Great Black Swamp: historical tales of 19th century northwest Ohio* published in 1999. Some persons and events referred to only briefly in this book were detailed in the first book.

I would like to acknowledge all those involved in preserving and telling the history of northwest Ohio. Of particular help in providing material for this volume were the Ottawa County Historical Society, the Lucas County/Maumee Valley Historical Society, the Fulton County Historical Society, Toledo Area Metroparks, the Toledo-Lucas County Public Library's Local History and Genealogy Department, and the Center for Archival Collections at Bowling Green State University.

As in the first book, access to a statewide borrowing system through the University of Toledo was an invaluable resource as was the *Northwest Ohio Quarterly*, an historical journal for over 70 years. If it happened in the history of northwest Ohio it likely has been written about, at some point, in the *Quarterly*. Thanks is due as well to Marilyn Ziegman of Fostoria who provided the writings of her ancestor, Samuel Skinner, and to H. Lee Dunn and Charter One Bank in downtown Toledo. Special thanks is also due to my wife Denise for all her support and her proofreading and editing skills.

As much as possible I aimed for accuracy, relying on written versions of events, many penned over 100 years ago. But recorded history is filled with honest mistakes, subjective interpretation, and at times fabrication, or as the French writer Guy de Maupassant once observed: "History, that excitable and lying old lady."

# CHAPTER I

## FALLEN TIMBERS TALES

*Author's Note: For nearly 40 years prior to the Battle of Fallen Timbers, the Ohio frontier had at times resembled a war zone. The Indians vowed to keep white settlers from crossing north over the Ohio River while the settlers, voracious in their desire for more land, kept coming. Continuous and increasingly violent clashes took place between the two groups as they raided back and forth over the Ohio River. Atrocities on both sides were the norm, with mercy the exception.*

*After the American Revolution, the settlers demanded the young and weak United States government provide protection, and President George Washington attempted to comply. An army led by General Josiah Harmar raided Miami Indian villages in present-day Fort Wayne, Indiana in October, 1790 and marched right into a series of ambushes, suffering heavy losses. A year later a second army, under General Arthur St. Clair, marched along the Wabash River near present-day Fort Recovery, Ohio. They made camp on November 3, 1791, believing there were only a few Indians in the area. Waiting for them in the nearby woods, however, were over 1,000 armed and ready warriors from eight tribes.*

*The Indians struck at dawn the next day and when the smoke had cleared over 600 of St. Clair's troops lay dead on the ground with hundreds more wounded or missing. Dazed and bleeding survivors fled, limping and stumbling back toward Cincinnati. At the battlefield, the dead lay silent, their mouths stuffed with dirt, Indian scorn for men who had taken so much land and wanted still more.*

*It was the worst defeat ever of an American army by Indians. The number of dead soldiers along that bloody river that day was more than twice the number that would fall at Custer's much better known defeat at Little Big Horn 85 years later. Panic swept over the Ohio frontier and President Washington knew he had a serious problem. It would be nearly three years before another army would dare to return to the area.*

*Blood in the Sand*

August 20, 1794. The Maumee Valley. The peaceful sound of raindrops splashing on water rose from the Maumee River before dawn that morning as two large but very different armies slept, one Native, the other American. Though separated physically by only a few miles, insurmountable walls divided them culturally. As the darkness melted into a gray dawn, an occasional but ominous rumble of thunder echoed down the Maumee Valley.

The Indians had been gathering in present-day Maumee much of the summer. It had been nearly three years since they had given the Americans a whipping and they were anxious to give them another. The Americans, tired from three weeks of marching and building a chain of supply forts, had arrived in the area a couple of days earlier from Fort Defiance and camped in the bluffs above Roche de Boeuf in present-day Waterville. There they built a temporary fort named Camp Deposit and readied themselves for battle.

The Americans were led by an ill-tempered general named Anthony Wayne, a veteran of the Revolution, and given to attacks of gout. He had been called out of retirement by President Washington to do what two previous generals could not do: defeat the Indians in battle on the Ohio frontier and open the lands north of the Ohio River to white settlement.

Anthony Wayne was not President Washington's first choice. Vain, self-promoting and often disliked by fellow officers, he had been given the nickname "Mad Anthony" sometime during the Revolution, although its origins remain murky. But he had distinguished himself in battle during the Revolution and did have qualities that suited him to lead a distant, frontier campaign; that of a conservative strategist and strict discipli-

*Anthony Wayne's march from July 28th to August 20th, 1794.*

*This wall mural gives an artist's view of The Battle of Fallen Timbers. The large mural, which is in the Charter One Bank in downtown Toledo, was painted by Ettore Caser in 1930. (Photo courtesy of Charter One Bank).*

narian. Indeed, it was not uncommon for Wayne to give the soldiers under his command sentences of death by hanging or firing squad or whippings of 100 lashes, which frequently meant a lingering and agonizing death.

Wayne also strongly believed that any treaty negotiations taking place with the Indians had to be done from the standpoint of unquestioned military superiority, which also appealed to President Washington. Beginning in 1792 he had recruited an army of some 4,000 soldiers, known officially as the Legion of the United States, from the cities and, in some cases, jails of the East Coast and moved slowly but methodically west, marching and training. He reached Fort Washington in Cincinnati in May, 1793 and by the end of that year had moved to Fort Green Ville, now Greenville, Ohio, only about 60 miles north, where he spent the winter. He had no intention of meeting the Indians in battle until he felt absolutely ready. Not only did he want to win, he deeply wanted a chance to assure himself a place in history.

Now on a rainy sunrise in the latter part of the summer of 1794, Anthony Wayne was about to get that chance. Standing in his way were around 1,400 Indians from at least seven tribes. One of them was Chief Little Turtle, leader of the Miami tribe, the mastermind behind the defeats of the American armies in 1790 and 1791, and ostensibly the leader in the upcoming fight.

However as the battle drew nigh it was a gloomy Little Turtle who walked about the plains above the Maumee River, a leader wise enough to see the larger picture. He had led an unsuccessful attack on Fort Recovery at the end of June, an event that both exposed flaws in Indian strategies and revealed the strength of this new American army.

At a tribal council a couple of days prior to the battle Little Turtle is reported to have said, "We have beaten the enemy twice under different commanders. We cannot expect the same good fortune to attend us always. The Americans are now led by a chief who never sleeps. Like the blacksnake, the day and night are alike to him for during all the time he has been marching on our villages, nonwithstanding the watchfulness of our young men, we have not been able to surprise him."

Little Turtle closed his speech with a call to listen to Anthony Wayne's peace overtures and a warning that the Great Spirit would be angry if the path of war was chosen over the path of peace. His words were met with a stony silence by the other chiefs and his rival, Chief Blue Jacket of the Shawnees, said to him, "has my brother turned coward?" Stung by the inference, Little Turtle said no more.

Then Blue Jacket seized the moment and gave a passionate speech vowing to make Anthony Wayne "walk a bloody path." Thus he became the Indian leader at the Battle of Fallen Timbers. Little Turtle agreed to fight, but only as leader of his Miami clan.

In spite of Little Turtle's reservations, the Indians were generally confident going into the battle. Having defeated an American army twice before, they were at the height of their power. They had a large and battle-hardened force of their own. And the British, who occupied Fort Miamis about three miles downstream, had promised their support. In fact, ready to fight alongside the Indians were about 60 Canadian militia.

Another aspect contributing to Native confidence was an overriding belief that Manitou, or Great Spirit, was watching over them and would guide them to victory. For the Americans were coming to take away their lands and ultimately their very existence. This was not a geo-political dispute over ideology and territory. It was to be a battle of right versus wrong, good versus evil. Losing was unthinkable.

But the rain that fell early the morning of August 20th would play an important role as it delayed the movement of Wayne's Legion a couple of hours. By around 7 a.m. they had left Camp Deposit and were under way, Wayne's gout being so bad that day he had to be lifted onto his horse. Many of the Indians, however, who had been fasting in preparation for battle, figured the rain ruled out a fight in the morning if not for the whole day and went back to Fort Miamis or their Swan Creek camps in present-day downtown Toledo for food. In fact many had been fasting for two or three days expecting the attack to have come sooner than it did and were quite hungry.

The rest of the Indian force, around 1,000 of the original 1,400, was stretched in a line across a morass of logs, trees knocked down by a tornado or windstorm several years earlier, a field that would come to be known to history as Fallen Timbers. In between the fallen trees, high grass, brush and saplings grew, creating a thick entanglement.

Around 9 a.m. the sun had burned off the clouds and about 800 Legion troops, backed up by 1,500 Kentucky militia, continued to advance on horse and by foot toward the Fallen Timbers battlefield in five parallel columns spread about 200 yards apart. Leading the way on what had become a sultry, summer morning were two Kentucky privates, Sherman Moore and William Steele, selected for the honor of leading the Legion.

At around 10 a.m., after advancing about 100 yards into the area of downed trees, the well-concealed Indian force opened fire, sending young Moore and Steele to their eternal rewards, and throwing the American advance into chaos. Miami and Delaware warriors rose in a line and fired, then dropped to the ground to reload while second and third lines did the same.

The air filled with smoke and the roar of gunfire, the shouts of men, and the screams of terrified and wounded horses. The American advance troops were soon in retreat while a portion of the Indians pursued. "Everything is confusion," a captain shouted to a general. If at any point in the battle the Indians could have broken through the American lines it was then.

But the Indians were not at maximum strength and only a portion pursued the troops while the rest remained at the fallen timbers site. Some of the pursuing warriors were armed only with tomahawks and knives while all the Americans had rifles. Their offensive line was now stretched over too much territory and their pursuit led them into the main body of the Legion where its training and superior firepower began to take its toll. At this point in the battle, Blue Jacket's whereabouts are unknown.

A little over a half hour into the battle Anthony Wayne gave the order to fire then charge the Indians with fixed bayonets before the warriors could reload and fire. With no apparent leader or tactical plan in place, the Indians were soon in a disorganized retreat.

"We could not stand against the sharp end of their guns and we ran to the river, swamps and thickets and to the islands in the river covered with corn," a Native leader later reported.

"Our moccasins trickled blood in the sand and the water was red in the river."

What both sides had presumed would be a tumultuous battle was over in a little more than an hour. By 11 a.m. most of the firing had stopped. So brief was the battle some American officers suspected the retreat was a ruse designed to lure the soldiers into a trap, but this was not to be.

The Indians raced for Fort Miamis where the British had promised the protection of their fort if needed. There, perhaps, they could get reorganized and mount a counteroffensive. However they were stunned to find the gates of the fort barred, their supposed allies fearing an attack by the Americans if they were allowed in.

The retreat continued down the Maumee River to Swan Creek where many of the Indians had their camps and their families. Once there, "we were no longer strong like braves and warriors but like women weak and afraid," an Indian fighter recalled years later. "Many of our young men knew the Great Spirit was angry and would not help them." Little Turtle's prophecy had been realized.

The battle over, Anthony Wayne set his sights on Fort Miamis where the hated Union Jack he had fought against in the Revolution was flapping in the breeze. He encamped within sight of the fort to taunt the British while he decided what to do next. He very much wanted a fight with them and had the authority from the War Department to do so. The fort, completed earlier in the year, was actually on territory ceded by the British to the United States in the 1783 treaty ending the Revolution.

At one point Wayne allegedly ordered a soldier to fetch a bucket of water from the Maumee River right below the fort. When the soldier replied that the British would probably shoot him, Wayne said, "that's the very thing I want them to do, John. Let them kill you and we'll massacre every soul of 'em."

After hanging around a couple of days–Wayne at one point rode within pistol shot of the fort– and exchanging insulting letters with the British commandant, Wayne decided it was not worth the military risk and he and his Legion packed up and left on August 23rd. They marched back up the Maumee

River to Fort Defiance, torching Indian villages and crops along the way.

Meanwhile, back at the Swan Creek camps, the mood was one of despair. The Indians, who had expected a great battle and victory, had instead been slapped aside in what was little more than a skirmish. The end of summer was fast approaching, valuable hunting time had been lost, crops and villages had been burned, and the prospect of starvation in the coming winter loomed large.

The historical importance of the clash that came to be known as The Battle of Fallen Timbers was not realized by its participants at the time. The Americans suffered 33 dead and about 100 wounded while the Indians were believed to have lost 40 or 50, including four Canadians, with at least 100 wounded.

The battle's significance, however, became apparent the following fall and winter when small groups of Indians, including high profile chiefs like Blue Jacket, began approaching American forts waving the white flag of surrender. Anthony Wayne was now "The Wind" to the Indians as he had knocked down everything before him.

Wayne's victory had established the unquestioned military superiority President Washington wanted and given a young United States of America de facto control of the Ohio frontier. This would open up the Northwest Territory for settlement, thus paving the way for an enormous change in the cultural landscape. Now all that was needed was the paperwork.

### The Treaty of Green Ville

After the battle Anthony Wayne remained a couple of weeks at Fort Defiance. There he wrote to the Secretary of War, "It's with infinite pleasure that I now announce to you the brilliant success of the Federal army under my command..." He then marched to the headwaters of the Maumee River where he built Fort Wayne which was named after him. In early November he returned to Fort Green Ville to spend the winter and the troops of the fort gave him a hero's welcome as he and his soldiers marched through the gate.

Waiting for him also at Green Ville was a delegation of Wyandot Indians who told him they were "determined to bury the hatchet and scalping knife deep in the ground." And as the climactic year of 1794 drew to a close, more groups of Natives approached Fort Green Ville and the other forts in the region. Having been defeated in battle, abandoned by the British, and now caught in the grip of a long, dark winter of want, they were a beaten people.

In January Anthony Wayne announced that a general treaty council would be held at Fort Green Ville beginning June 15th. Any doubts he had about Indian cooperation were eased on February 7th when the Shawnee Chief Blue Jacket rode into the fort with a delegation of both Shawnee and Delaware warriors. Blue Jacket assured Wayne he would convince the other Shawnee chiefs and sub chiefs, still angry and bitter about the defeat, to agree to the treaty council. Wayne in turn gave him an officer's coat which he wore proudly.

As the winter continued, Anthony Wayne instructed the commanders of the various forts in the region to issue food to the hungry Indians showing up. While he was not fond of the idea of subsidizing his recent enemies he knew that to do so was in the best interest of his ultimate goal: to have a peace treaty signed by the major chiefs of the region.

The winter melted into spring and, after the crops were planted, members of various tribes in early June began drifting into Fort Green Ville. Anthony Wayne had constructed a sizable council house on the grounds of the fort and went out of his way to see to it that his Indians guests felt comfortable and at ease, and food, drink, and gifts were distributed. Due to the lateness of several tribes, the actual negotiations started a month late on July 15th. By that time there were over 1100 Indians from ten tribes at the fort.

Of all the chiefs present only Little Turtle of the Miami tribe engaged Anthony Wayne in any serious debate, at times seeing through his motives and putting him on the defensive. But the other chiefs were almost unanimously agreeing with Wayne's proposals as they were presented, especially the influential Blue Jacket who may have cut a side deal with him— Blue Jacket was later granted a $300 yearly subsidy. Thus Wayne was able to isolate the Miami leader and overcome his objections.

*The original painting (also shown on the back cover), The Treaty of Greene Ville by Howard Chandler Christy, hangs in the State Capitol Building in Columbus. Standing, Miami Chief Little Turtle presents a wampum belt to Anthony Wayne. The hatless soldier standing behind Anthony Wayne is Lieutenant William Henry Harrison, Wayne's aide during the Battle of Fallen Timbers and later commander of Fort Meigs during the War of 1812 and elected president of the United States in 1840. Seated behind Little Turtle in long sleeves and facing outward is the Shawnee Chief Blue Jacket, leader of the Native-American forces at Fallen Timbers.(Reproduced by permission of the Ohio Historical Society).*

As Anthony Wayne was negotiating within the walls of his own fort with people he had beaten in battle less than a year earlier and surrounded by a large army, it was his game to win. One Potawatomi chief told Wayne, "you may depend on our sincerity." He then added, "we cannot but be sincere as your forts will be planted thick among us."

One by one the ten articles of the treaty were agreed to and on August 3rd, the signing began. In exchange for cash annuities and goods, the Indians had given up claim to approximately two-thirds of what would become the state of Ohio. A reluctant Little Turtle eventually signed the treaty, saying he was the last to sign it and would be the last to break it. Little Turtle was actually the 77th signee. Anthony Wayne had won the war and now had won the peace, and his place in history was assured.

Ninety Indians, primarily chiefs, signed the Treaty of Greenville. Fifty years later, there may not have been that many full-blooded Natives left in the entire state of Ohio.

*The Backstabbing Second*

In all human endeavors, it seems, human pettiness and politics are present to some degree. It was certainly no different in Anthony Wayne's Ohio campaign.

Wayne had more than just attacking Indians, daily command decisions, and a harsh frontier environment to deal with. He had an intensely jealous and resentful second in command, General James Wilkinson, questioning and undermining his plans and decisions along the way and encouraging other officers to do the same.

This frontier soap opera was recorded in a daily journal *From Green Ville to Fallen Timbers,* that chronicles the Wayne campaign from July 28th to September 14th in the fateful year of 1794. The author remains unknown to this day although it had to be a senior officer privy to the inner circles of command. The diary is favorable to Wilkinson and so unfavorable to Anthony Wayne, some historians think Wilkinson himself was the one who penned it, or dictated to an aide.

The journal describes the daily events of the army's march north from Fort Green Ville to the confluence of the Maumee and Auglaize rivers where it built Fort Defiance; its journey down the Maumee River valley to the Battle of Fallen Timbers; and its subsequent return to Fort Defiance.

It begins on the day the Americans departed from Fort Green Ville and almost immediately criticizes Anthony Wayne's marching plans, quoting a captain as saying, "a Board of the ablest officers in Europe or in the world, were they employed for the purpose, could not have designated an order of march more absurd, feeble, or defenceless."

The August 1st entry continues to criticize the order of march and credits General Wilkinson for "the safety of the Camp and of the Legion–yet not withstanding the zeal and promptitude hitherto displayed by him, in his public character, in offering honestly and cheerfully every aid, information, and advice..."

On August 3rd there was an unusual event. Anthony Wayne was resting in his tent in mid-afternoon when a large tree fell on it. Wayne "escaped, by about six inches, being mashed to Death by the Body of the tree." Wayne reportedly had no pulse when dragged from his tent but was revived with a jolt of whiskey.

On August 4th the author is so disturbed with Anthony Wayne's handling of the march thus far that he tells another officer he wished the Indians would come and tomahawk him to prevent him from cutting his own throat. The army was now slogging across part of the Great Black Swamp.

Four days later upon reaching the confluence of the Maumee and Auglaize rivers, Wilkinson received an order from Anthony Wayne to ford the Maumee. "He obeyed it," the journal noted, "considering himself subject to the commands of a Despot who consults no consideration of delicacy, of propriety, of justice or of professional principles."

On August 10th Wilkinson's feelings were apparently bruised as Anthony Wayne "passed Gen'l Wilkinson's tent within ten steps three times without looking at him altho' he was at breakfast and in full view."

Five days later, the building of Fort Defiance complete, the army went on the march down the Maumee River and the journal again paints a gloomy picture of things; "Our situation become hourly more alarming–it is indeed fearful–but the

C in C (Wayne) will receive no advice and the state of his health exasperates his naturally bad temper." Anthony Wayne was suffering from a flare-up of his chronic gout.

On August 18th the army arrived at Roche de Boeuf and established Camp Deposit where the journal observed, "we continue perfectly ignorant of the C in Cs plan for the Campaign and are at a loss for the principles on which he acts–the protection of providence may save him–nothing else can."

The August 20th entry, by far the longest in the journal, gives a large amount of detail on the Battle of Fallen Timbers mixed with criticism of Anthony Wayne's tactics and general handling of the battle. The overall tone of the entry is that the American victory that day was the stuff of miracles.

On August 23rd Anthony Wayne ordered a funeral ceremony complete with cannon fire to honor the dead prior to marching back up the Maumee River. The ceremony "constituted a pageant so truly ridiculous as to excite the derision of every person of observation or candor," according to the journal.

Two days later as the army neared Fort Defiance the drumbeat of criticism of Wayne continued along with the observation, "still fortune, the blind goddess favours us–heaven grant a continuance–for in her smiles consists our main dependence." On August 27th, the day before arriving back at Fort Defiance, the journal notes that General Wilkinson "has been insulted in his feelings and wounded in his dignity" by Anthony Wayne conveying orders to him through a junior officer.

On September 1st, "the C in C preaches vigilance and caution but practises none–dined with him today–the conversation as usual turned on the Battle which seems an inexhaustible subject." Four days later Anthony Wayne's successes are again attributed to luck–"Happy man, whose folly and incapacity is remedied by a concurrence of fortunate contingencies equally improbable and unexpected!"

On September 10th Wayne is excoriated once again; "what levity, irritability, and want of circumspection does this little great man daily betray." The journal ends on September 14th when Anthony Wayne left Fort Defiance for the headwaters of the Maumee River to build Fort Wayne.

If the author of the journal was not General Wilkinson it

certainly was an officer firmly in his camp. It is said that half of Anthony Wayne's officers were fully behind him with the rest either behind Wilkinson or unable to make up their mind. Anthony Wayne was aware of Wilkinson's disloyalty but generally chose to ignore it until the more important affairs of battle and treaty negotiations were concluded. At the time of his death in 1796, Wayne was preparing a case for the court-martial of General James Wilkinson. Among other things, he began to suspect that the tree that fell on his tent that nearly killed him may have had help from Wilkinson.

In later years it was confirmed what Wayne and others in the government had also suspected: that Wilkinson had been working as a paid secret agent for the Spanish government while serving as an American general–Spain still held territory on the continent. Denounced as "a double traitor" by Andrew Jackson, he died in 1825 and was buried in an unmarked grave in Mexico City. He is viewed in a dim light by American historians.

### Ohio Indian War Diary

Of the thousands of soldiers who took part in the Ohio Indian Wars, only a handful kept a diary or journal. One was by a major named John Buell. He was born in Connecticut in 1753, fought as a soldier in the Revolution and achieved officer's rank before that war ended in 1783. Ten years later he left civilian life and joined Anthony Wayne's Legion of the United States which was preparing for its Ohio campaign.

His original diary, whereabouts unknown, was crudely transcribed, edited and released by a New York publisher on an unknown date, probably in the 1800's. It was re-edited and transcribed by Richard C. Knopf, an editor and historian with the Anthony Wayne Parkway Board in Columbus and released in 1957.

The diary covers the period from March 25, 1793 to February 14, 1795 and gives an insider's view of both major and minor events of the Ohio campaign and of military life on the frontier. It begins simply on March 25th, 1793, "I left my children and friends to join the Army..."

Over the next several weeks Buell made his way to New

York, then Philadelphia, then Pittsburgh where Anthony Wayne and his Legion were camped 20 miles down the Ohio River. On April 19th he met with General Wayne and had dinner with him. John Buell was now Major Buell.

On May 6th the army broke camp for Fort Washington and Cincinnati where an uneventful summer was spent waiting to hear the results of treaty offers being made to the Indians. On September 10th when it was learned that Indians would not negotiate, Anthony Wayne began marching his large army north with Buell as one of his command officers.

In October one of the marching detachments of soldiers was attacked by Indians. A squadron of dragoons [calvary] retreated instead of following their officers in pursuit and two sergeants were killed in the fight. A furious Anthony Wayne decided to make a point. He ordered the arrest of the soldiers and the court-martial of the leader of the retreat. He also ordered the leader's grave to be dug who was subsequently found guilty and ordered to be shot. However Wayne used the opportunity to harangue an assembly of all the troops for a good half hour, then pardoned the leader and forgave the others.

In November the army arrived in what is now Darke County and built Fort Green Ville, the army's headquarters for the winter. In December a large detachment went north to what is now Fort Recovery, Ohio, site of the massive defeat of General Arthur St. Clair's army just over two year earlier. There they had the grisly task of collecting and burying the remains, including some four to five hundred skulls.

New Year's Day, 1794 was a festive one for Major Buell as he, Anthony Wayne, and a number of other officers traveled to Fort Jefferson, a nearby outpost. The extensive bill of fare there included venison, roast beef, mutton, turkey, all manner of game animals, vegetables, breads, desserts, and "plenty of the best of wine." They all returned to Fort Green Ville that night a bit heavier than when they left.

January was uneventful until Stiff Knee, an Indian allied with the American side, committed suicide, reportedly because he feared Anthony Wayne would make peace instead of war. "His death is much lamented," Buell wrote, "most of the officers of the army attended the funeral, fired cannon over his grave..."

In the latter part of February the morning quiet was disturbed by gunshots as two young officers, Lieutenants Hustin and Bradshaw, had fought each other in a duel. Dueling was still a common practice in those days. They had fired simultaneously and both were mortally wounded. "They were two promising officers," Buell wrote, "Bradshaw in particular. He was a man of great genius and excellent education, was bred to the law, but drink was his failing; it seems that the dispute began in this way. They were friends before."

They were buried in full uniform side-by-side although Anthony Wayne would not allow any artillery salute. It would seem that the frontier winter was taking its toll on morale and discipline as Major Buell wrote, "about this time there was the most quarreling, jargon, and confusion throughout the whole legion that I ever knew in any army."

March and April were rife with rumors of renewed war with England which would mean the army would march back to defend the East Coast, an appealing prospect. On April 21st Buell penned, "all the talk in camp is that the legion will be called to the Atlantic States, we are much flattered with the prospect of getting out of these woods." Three days later another duel was fought and another young lieutenant lay mortally wounded, shot in the head.

As the weather warmed so did the action as Indians were now attacking supply convoys and troops moving between Fort Green Ville and Fort Washington in Cincinnati. In mid-May Major Buell left Fort Green Ville with 200 men to reinforce a convoy marching to Green Ville that had been under Indian attack, returning safely on May 20th.

The rest of the early and mid summer saw Buell in charge of expeditions to gather hay to feed the large number of cattle, horses and mules of the Legion. This was dangerous work, at times taking him several miles from the safety of the fort. He summed up his work on July 12th: "I completed the haying and got 715 loads, brought it to this garrison and stacked it. I had a long laborious tour but was very fortunate, lost no men nor no other accident. We had a number of alarms..."

On July 14th another duel was fought and another lieutenant lay dead. The argument this time was over a horse. It was about this time Anthony Wayne told the Legion to prepare to march north at any time. However on July 26th he told Major Buell that he would remain behind as commander of Fort Green Ville.

On July 28th Anthony Wayne and much of the Legion left for its eventual destiny at Fallen Timbers. The next day Buell assessed the mixed group left behind now under his command. "I found I had 520 regular soldiers, 12 Kentucky volunteers (left sick), 73 women, 23 children, 30 Choctaw Indians, 5 warriors and 2 squaws, prisoners, making in the whole 600 and 65..."

On August 20th, the day guns roared in the Maumee Valley, things were considerably more peaceful at Fort Green Ville. "I have completed the fence around my turnips which are all sowed," Buell wrote. "We grow impatient to hear from the army. We know not where they are or what has become of them..."

Nine days later Major Buell received his first hint that a battle had been fought. "Some of the Choctaw Indians came in and (as we understand them) there has been an action but they cannot talk English and we have no interpreter. Just at night some more came in, one of them can speak English, and he says there has been a great fight and that General Wayne has driven them all off beyond the British fort..."

Things began to tense in September as many of the Indians that had gone north to fight at Fallen Timbers were returning to the area. On the 15th Buell noted, "my spies come in and report that they see great signs of Indians in different directions."

On October 12th Buell wrote, "For three nights I have slept very little, expecting that the wagons [a large convoy on its way from Fort Hamilton] are attacked, or one of the garrisons ought to be attacked..."

On October 28th the last of the Kentucky volunteers, traditionally a difficult lot, left the fort for home. "The last of the Kentucky volunteers left this day except a few left sick which rids me of a good deal of trouble," a relieved Buell noted.

November 2nd became a day of celebration as Anthony

Wayne and his army returned triumphantly to Fort Green Ville. "When the General got within about a half a mile we commenced firing with both cannon and continued until he got within the fort. The troops of the garrison then gave him three cheers." The returning army responded with cannon salutes and three cheers of their own and a gill of whiskey [about four ounces] was ordered for all the soldiers.

On December 8th Major Buell left Fort Green Ville in command of a large supply convoy for Fort Wayne. The next day as they neared Fort Recovery, site of General St. Clair's 1791 defeat, "we found skull bones scattered through the woods for 15 miles before we got to the Fort....there was as much as three wagon loads of bones that had been collected and buried [the previous year] yet they were lying thick on the ground."

Buell and his convoy made it to Fort Wayne in four days with no major incidents. On the return trip home weather would be a factor. On the second night a cold and hard rain fell all night. The next morning as the wet and miserable group trudged on "the wind shifted to the north-west and all at once became as dark as night and a most tremendous hurricane came on that I have ever seen, [the] falling of trees was like an action with small arms." The soldiers ran to a grove of trees and waited out the storm. While none were hurt "the scare was dreadful," Buell noted.

On New Year's Day 1795 talk of peace had replaced talk of war at Fort Green Ville. During the month of December, a number of Indians had come though the gates of the fort carrying white flags. And Anthony Wayne had just received a letter from the commander at Fort Wayne saying that Indians from four different tribes had come there seeking peace and were on their way to Fort Green Ville to meet with him. The day was celebrated with dining and an evening fireworks display with Major Buell noting, "peace with the Indians is the conversation in general."

On January 20th some Miami warriors arrived with two women prisoners they had taken in St. Clair's defeat. It was a joyous reunion for one of the women as her husband was a Fort Green Ville soldier. There were now quite a large number of Indians at the fort, chiefs in particular.

THE GREAT BLACK SWAMP II:

Major John Buell's diary ends unremarkably on February 14th, 1795. "The Shawnees and Delawares went home. Blue Jacket was elegantly arrayed with a scarlet coat, two gold epaulets, a good wollen shirt and his other dress compared. He had a sister with him arrayed equal with himself .The chief of the Delawares was dressed in the same uniform as Blue Jacket but wore no epaulet. We have no news from any other quarter."

*Chief Blue Jacket*

*Author's Note: The following account is based on the book "Blue Jacket: War Chief of the Shawnees" written by John Bennett, and published by the Ross County (Ohio) Historical Society in 1943. One of the premises of the book is that Blue Jacket was a Caucasian prisoner named Marmaduke Van Swearingen who was captured in 1769 at the age of 17 in the hills of western Pennsylvania and adopted into the Shawnee tribe. The only other major work done on Blue Jacket, Alan Eckert's 1969 book of the same title, proceeds with the same premise.*

*However according to newspaper reports, recent DNA testing done on descendants of both Blue Jacket and Marmaduke Van Swearingen has indicated, but not definitively proven, that Blue Jacket was of Native-American heritage. And one descendant of Blue Jacket living in Oklahoma has denounced the characterization of him being white as "a lie." It's possible the issue will never be resolved satisfactorily, especially in light of the fact that the Shawnee chief has been dead nearly 200 years and his place of burial is unknown.*

Little is known about Blue Jacket's early years. In 1773 there was an Indian village known as Blue Jacket's Town on Deer Creek in southern Ohio near present day Chillicothe. The town was described by a passing missionary; "The buildings are of logs; their number about twelve...It is a peaceable town." At this time Blue Jacket was married to a white woman who had been taken prisoner and she had given birth to a son. However, when a 1774 treaty called for both sides to return all prisoners, Blue Jacket's wife returned to visit her family in Virginia and never came back. She was pregnant when she left and gave birth to a daughter, Nancy Blue Jacket. She eventually married and became Nancy Stewart, a name that will come into play later.

Throughout the 1770's and into the 1780's when the Ohio River valley was a hotbed of conflict between the Indians and whites, Blue Jacket's name does not come up often. However he was believed to be present at a prisoner exchange in 1787 when he and several other Shawnee chiefs waited on the banks of the Ohio River opposite Limestone, Kentucky. There they met with Daniel Boone, highly respected by the Indians, and a feast was held after the exchange to celebrate. The next day Blue Jacket spent the day hunting with Boone's son. This relationship would prove to be valuable.

About a year later Blue Jacket led a small party of Shawnees into Kentucky on a horse-stealing expedition, stole eight or nine, and fled back toward Ohio. They were overtaken by pursuing Kentuckians and the group scattered with all escaping but Blue Jacket. He pointed toward the direction of Maysville, Kentucky, where Daniel Boone had a trading post, and asked to be taken to him for judgment and his captors agreed.

Boone was probably disappointed to see his son's hunting companion in such a predicament but he saw to it that Blue Jacket was tied and locked in a cabin for the night. However someone, by accident or design, had left a hunting knife sticking from the wall. Blue Jacket was able to squirm over and get the knife, cut his ties, then hack his way through the door, escaping just before dawn.

His captors pursued him but found only his deerskin leggings he had thrown off in order to run faster. Several days later he limped into his Shawnee village nearly naked, badly scratched and exhausted. He let his young braves know in no uncertain terms that they would from now on do their horse-stealing elsewhere.

By 1778 Blue Jacket had moved his town north into what is now Logan County as the Indians were slowly being squeezed out of southern Ohio. Through the 1780's Blue Jacket continued to rise in stature and by 1790, through his ability and the deaths of other chiefs, he was now the leader of the Shawnee nation.

That year saw the beginning of a climactic five-year period.

In October Blue Jacket was an important leader in the attacks on the army of General Josiah Harmar which had marched from Cincinnati to burn the Indian villages and crops at the headwaters of the Maumee River where Fort Wayne now stands. While the Americans achieved their objective, with the loss of nearly 200 men and all their horses and cannon, the event became known as Harmar's Defeat.

A little over a year later Blue Jacket was second in command when the army of General Arthur St. Clair was resoundingly defeated on November 4, 1791 at present-day Fort Recovery, Ohio with a loss of over 600 men. By then Blue Jacket had moved his village north again to the confluence of the Maumee and Auglaize rivers where the city of Defiance now stands.

Blue Jacket's next, and last, major military moment would not come for nearly three years when he became the leader of Indian forces at the Battle of Fallen Timbers when Little Turtle stepped aside. While the event was a tide-turning loss for the Indians, Blue Jacket, to his credit, gave it his best shot.

In 1795 Blue Jacket was a leading spokesman for peace in the months leading up to the Treaty of Greenville and during the actual negotiations, perhaps prompted by a generous subsidy awarded him. After 1795, little is known about Blue Jacket. A map of Indian villages in 1810 shows a Blue Jacket village on the Detroit River about mid-way between present-day Monroe and downtown Detroit, Michigan.

It was about that time the Shawnee leader Tecumseh was marshaling Indian forces for one last fight against the Americans. Whether he approached Blue Jacket is not known, only that if he did, Blue Jacket declined.

In May, 1813 a land grant was made in Logan County, Ohio to "Nancy Stewart, daughter of Blue Jacket, by the chief of the Shawnee tribes then located at Wapakonetta." From this it can be inferred that Blue Jacket was still alive and living back in Ohio and that he had secured land for his daughter. The next, and last, reference to Blue Jacket came again in a Logan County record in 1824: "There is granted by the United States to Nancy Stewart, daughter of the late Shawnee chief, one section of land."

So Blue Jacket may have died between 1813 and 1824 although some accounts place his death in 1810. Exactly when or where he died or where he was laid to rest are unknown. What is known is that he was a participant in, and witness to, many important events in the dynamic final decades of the 18th century in Ohio. Unfortunately, too little is known about him.

### Fort Defiance Heartbreak

There was a youth named John Brickell of Pittsburgh who was captured by Delaware Indians near his home in February, 1791. He endured a long and arduous march to the Delaware village at the confluence of the Maumee and Auglaize rivers, now the site of Defiance. There he was adopted by one of the Delawares, Whingwypooshies, and became part of his family.

Life was good in the Delaware village and Brickell and Whingwypooshies became very close, the lad becoming a skilled hunter. Then one morning in August, 1794 an Indian messenger raced into camp and told them to run for their lives as Anthony Wayne and his army were on the march down the Auglaize River. Brickell and the rest of the tribe fled with little more than the clothes on their backs, barely escaping the bullets of the advance soldiers.

They camped on Swan Creek where, in the aftermath of Fallen Timbers, they spent a long, hungry winter. In the spring the Delawares traveled back upriver to Fort Defiance to make peace with the Americans. It was an apprehensive journey for Whingwypooshies as he knew that any agreement with the Americans would call for the release of prisoners on both sides, meaning he could lose his new son. The matter weighed heavily on Brickell's mind as well as he had become attached to his new family but still had longings for his old one.

As they neared the fort, "the children hung round me crying and asked me if I was going to leave them. I told them I did not know," Brickell recalled. Later, at the fort, Whingwypooshies begged him to stay. "You have lived long with me, you have hunted for me but our treaty says you must be free. If you choose to go with the people of your own color, I have no right to say a word; but if you choose to stay with me your people have no right to speak."

"I was silent a few minutes," Brickell remembered, "during which time it seemed as if I thought of almost everything–of the children I had just left crying–of the Indians I was attached to, and I thought of my people, which I remembered and this latter thought predominated and I said 'I will go with my kin.'"

Whingwypooshies was crushed. "I have raised you; I have learned you how to hunt. You are a good hunter; you have been better to me than my own sons. I am now getting old and cannot hunt...I leaned upon you as on a staff but now it is broken. You are going to leave me and I have no right to say a word...I am ruined."

"He then sank back, in tears, to his seat," Brickell recalled. "I heartily joined him in his tears, parted with him, and have never seen or heard of him since."

*The Man With Two Graves*

After the Treaty of Greenville, Anthony Wayne attended to various duties in the area and in mid-November, 1796 was sailing across Lake Erie to inspect the military outpost at Presque Isle (Erie, PA) when seized with an acute case of gout. He was taken ashore there and an intestinal disorder aggravated his condition.

He lay in great pain for nearly a month. On December 14th, a member of the outpost wrote, "how long he can continue to suffer such torture is hard to say but it appears to me that nature must soon sink under such an acute affliction." The following day just as a doctor arrived from Pittsburgh, Anthony Wayne died at the age of 51. Per his instructions he was buried at the foot of the flagstaff of the fort. There he would rest in peace, for a while.

In 1809 his son, Colonel Isaac Wayne, came to retrieve his bones for proper burial in the family churchyard near Philadelphia. Upon opening the coffin he was dismayed to discover that his father's body was nearly perfectly preserved and far too much of a load to carry over the mountains of Pennsylvania.

So Isaac Wayne employed the services of a local cook to boil the body in a large kettle, separating the bones from the remaining soft tissues. It took some time but the macabre task was completed and the bones were taken to the family church-yard while the rest was reburied at the fort. Monuments to Anthony Wayne mark both burial sites, a man with two graves.

### The Second Battle of Fallen Timbers

For over 70 years the Fallen Timbers monument has stood on a Maumee bluff, the floodplain below sweeping to the Maumee River. There, gazing to the river, the statues of Anthony Wayne, a Native-American, and a settler stand guard over sacred ground. For in that floodplain, history was made on August 20, 1794, or so it was long believed.

However extensive study in recent years of battle accounts and of the area has indicated that the bulk of the Battle of Fallen Timbers was not fought on the floodplain but in woods north and east of the monument. A 1995 archeological dig in that area, now a mix of forest and farmland, unearthed musket balls, brass buttons, and bayonets.

The research led to calls for establishment of an historic park

*Anthony Wayne as he appears on the Fallen Timbers Monument, Maumee.*

on the 187-acre site which led to a sort of second Battle of Fallen Timbers. The owners of the land, the City of Toledo, had plans to sell the land at top dollar to developers. And with appraisals of the value of the parcel differing to the tune of well over three million dollars and no clear financing on the part of those wanting to preserve it, the possibility that such an historic site might be paved over loomed over the land.

Several years of political rhetoric followed with the usual charges and countercharges. But during this time the two sides inched closer together. And in the fall of 1999 Congress passed legislation making the land a National Historic Site which ended the development threat. On June 20, 2000, the first day of summer, an agreement was reached to sell the land to the Toledo Area Metroparks. Unlike the first, there were no losers in the second Battle of Fallen Timbers.

# CHAPTER II

THE EARLY MAUMEE VALLEY

Two rivers flow westward from the state of Ohio and wind their way to their eventual destination, Fort Wayne, Indiana. There the union of the St. Marys River from west central Ohio and the St. Joseph River from the northwestern part of the state gives birth to the Maumee River. From there this new river courses back to the east, carving a valley on its 100- mile journey to Lake Erie, a river of history and change.

For thousands of years aboriginal peoples called the river and valley home. But the Native-Americans of the Maumee Valley, like all the tribes in the continent, had no written language, no way of permanently recording their story. Their history was an oral one, passed down by tribal elders and chiefs by the light of smoky campfires. And like the smoke of those campfires, much of their story has long since drifted away with the wind.

So what kind of home was the Maumee Valley to its long-time inhabitants? Some early white writers left behind a glimpse. For the Indian, "the Maumee River was a delightful home and a secure retreat," one unknown early writer recorded. "Its banks were studded with their villages, its rich bottomlands covered with their corn, while their light canoes glided over a beautiful current which was at once a convenient highway and an exhaustless reservoir of food. Forest, stream and prairie produced, spontaneously, and in superabundance, game fish, fruits, nuts,–all things necessary to supply their simple wants."

The Maumee River and valley not only provided for its early dwellers, it did so against a backdrop of natural splendor. "This beautiful valley was to the Indian an enchanted ground," according to a history of the Maumee Valley published in 1858. "He never left it for the briefest period without regret or returned to it without delight. The gurgling of the river as it broke into rapids over the rifted rocks–the soughing of the wind through the mighty forests–the drumming of the partridge at mid-day, and the prolonged midnight howl of the wolf were sweeter music to his ears than he ever listened to elsewhere."

"The world contained no other spot which the Ottawas and Miamis had gathered so many endearments," the 1858 history continues. "Not only were they contented–they wer e delighted to dwell amid the varied scenery of River, Rock, and Island and, like the Arcadian shepherds, they refused until refusal was unavailing to abandon it to their enemies."

The beauty and bounty of the river and valley was a secret known only to the Indians and a handful of white explorers and trappers until the second week of August, 1794. It was then that Anthony Wayne marched his Legion down the Auglaize River to the Maumee River where he built Fort Defiance at the confluence. There, the soldiers were amazed by what they saw.

"This place far excels in beauty any in the western country and believed equaled by none in the Atlantic States," wrote a lieutenant. "Here are vegetables of every kind in abundance, and we have marched four or five miles in corn fields down the Oglaize, and there are not less than one thousand acres of corn..."

Gazing from Fort Defiance a soldier wrote, "there were large corn fields, and a large quantity Irish potatoes, Pumpkins beans cucumbers and simblings [cymlings, or summer squash] all in Great perfection."

Another soldier was similarly impressed: 'The Whole abound in plenty, produced by the extensive Corn-Fields and Gardens contiguous to our present Encampment. The flourishing state of the productions of this Country convinces me of the Fertility of the Soil, and its pleasantness is most surprisingly beautiful."

A few days later Wayne's troops marched down the Maumee River to Roche de Boeuf to camp and prepare for the Battle of Fallen Timbers. There, observing the great rock rising from the river, Lieutenant William Clark, later of Lewis and Clark fame, wrote simply, "we behold one of the most beautiful landscapes ever painted."

But this being a time of war it wasn't long before smoke hung thick over the river and valley. In the aftermath of the battle, Anthony Wayne's troops laid waste to the Indian cornfields, gardens and villages of the Maumee.

Despite the events at Fallen Timbers that year, the Maumee Valley returned to being a pastoral home for Native people for a time. The barrier of The Great Black Swamp that ran south from the river would slow white settlement and allow the valley to continue as a tribal home for another couple of decades or so. A judge named Jacob Burnet, who traveled through the valley during that time later wrote down his recollections.

"My yearly trips to Detroit from 1796 to 1802 made it necessary to pass through some of the Indian towns and convenient to visit many of them. Of course I had frequent opportunities of seeing thousands of them in their villages and at their hunting camps and of forming an acquaintance with some of their distinguished Chiefs. I have eaten and slept in their towns and partaken of their hospitality..."

"In journeying more recently through the State, in discharging my judicial duties, I sometimes passed over the ground on which I had seen towns filled with happy families of that devoted race without perceiving the smallest trace of what had once been there. All their ancient settlements on the route to Fort Defiance, and from thence to the foot of the rapids [Maumee city] had been broken up and deserted...It seemed almost impossible that in so short a period such an astonishing change could have taken place."

But astonishing change had taken place. The Native population was gone, replaced by a European usurper that had other plans for the land. The great forests of the Maumee Valley were cut down and the Great Black Swamp was drained. The drainage from the farm fields that took their place changed the color of the river from what history describes as coppery and clear to mud brown and cloudy. And the cities that have since sprouted in the valley have added their own degree of contamination.

To be sure, significant stretches of the Maumee River and valley remain as places of scenic beauty today. However its onetime Native inhabitants will always hold an advantage over those who have since come in their wake: it will never hold the beauty it did when they lived on it.

*The Maumee River as seen from the Maumee-Perrysburg Bridge. In the center is Ewing Island where Native-American corn once grew.*

# CHAPTER III

TRAILS OF TEARS

Two different worlds existed in northwest Ohio in the 1820's. For the settlers it was a time of optimism and hope with land to be had and dreams to be chased. For the Natives it was a time of quiet desperation. Defeated in war, crowded onto smaller pieces of land, and increasingly diminished by poverty and alcoholism, they had become strangers in their own land.

Then came the Indian Removal Act of 1830. This legislation meant that the Indians, whether they wanted to or not, were going to cede their remaining lands to the United States and move west of the Mississippi River. What had been happening in bits and pieces was now stated national policy.

Northwest Ohio and southeast Michigan still had a fair number of Indians living in it in 1830. Some lived out of sight in the woods while others lived on small reserves granted to them in previous treaties, treaties that were going to be broken. In Ohio there were Wyandots in what is now Wynadot County, Ottawas in the Maumee Valley, Potawatomis in what are now Fulton and Williams County in Ohio, and Shawnees in Auglaize County, to name some. Most of them enjoyed good relations with the white settlers of the area and problems between the two groups were few.

However after 1830, government treaty agents and commissioners soon began informing the tribes of the new law of the land, and that they, while they could, should negotiate their best deal and leave. In a typical deal a tribe or group would sign away their land for money, annuities, and goods and leave within a specified period of time, usually a year or two. Those who refused to leave would be marched west at gunpoint.

The Indians, of course, were opposed to the policy. So were some whites, religious leaders in particular. But the forces at work were too strong and the Indians were going to leave, one way or the other. While there are official government records of the transactions there are only scattered eyewitness accounts of the actual departures, actions that fit the modern day definition of ethnic cleansing.

One early Wood County settler who arrived in the spring 1837 witnessed such a departure although he doesn't give a year or name the tribe. Since a large number of Ottawas left in August, 1837, this could have been what he saw. "I have not forgotten the Indian calvacade that passed our cabin one bright summer afternoon," the settler wrote. "There were old and young, male and female, about 150 of them. They were on their way to the general rendezvous prepatory to their exodus. It was a pretty, but withal a melancholy sight."

No one in the column spoke as it passed by, the only sounds heard by the settler were the footfall of the horses and the tinkling of the bells around their necks. "Each knew and kept his or her place perfectly. Their file was in good order, their marching excellent...But they were taking their last look at, and final leave of their dearly loved resorts. Old, familiar camping grounds, around which clustered their brightest and happiest memories and dearest and most sacred of all, the graves of their fathers all were to be left, abandoned, forgotten forever. No one could look upon that silent troop...and even faintly realize what it meant to them, without being moved to pity on their behalf."

In the 1830's a Potawatomi clan still roamed present-day Fulton and Williams County in extreme northwest Ohio and Hillsdale County in southeast Michigan. They were led by Chief Bawbeese and moved back and forth between the two areas staying out of sight in the woods as much as possible hoping that somehow they could remain. When the subject of going west came up Bawbeese would say, "the Sioux kill me, the Sioux kill us all," referring to the Plains Indians who were usually quite hostile to newcomers. However in 1840 there came an army general and 150 soldiers and time had run out on the Bawbeese band.

As the Potawatomis were gathered by the troops, a Hillsdale County farmer witnessed the event. "We heard they were going and made haste to bid them farewell. We gathered mellons; as the Indian passed we gave one to each man. They were deeply effected upon leaving and many were the hearty handshakes given us. Bawbeese endeavored to retain his usual calmness but he betrayed much emotion. As he took my father's hand his eyes filled with tears and he seemed to choke. 'Maybe go, maybe fight' was all the expression he gave to his emotion and turning he went upon his way."

But there would be no fight. To fight at that point would have been suicide and the Potawatomis left forever under heavy guard for a central rendezvous point in Kalamazoo. "At the head of the column in an open buggy drawn by an Indian pony rode the elderly chief Bawbeese, his gun standing be-

*This stone in southeastern Hillsdale County, Michigan, marks the last camp of Chief Bawbeese and his Potawatomi band before they were forcibly marched west in 1840.*

tween his knees. One soldier on foot preceded the buggy; on each side marched another. The chief's sixty-year-old wife followed on a pony, guarded by a single trooper."

The rest of the tribe was stretched out in a column a half mile or more. "A few were on ponies but most were on foot. The warriors had rifles and mournful faces; the women appeared still more dejected with blankets drawn over their heads. Boys and girls, careless of the future, full of mischief and tricks, knew little of where they were going and romped heedlessly on their way."

Near the present town of Edgerton in southwest Williams County on the banks of the St. Joseph River lived another band of Potawatomi led by Chief Popquaw. Around 1838, soldiers came for them and lined them up to be marched away and some area settler families gathered to say goodbye.

Chief Popquaw stepped out of line to say farewell to the young daughter of a farm family he had befriended and a nervous soldier shot and killed him. There were some tense moments that followed as angry Indians and some whites confronted the soldiers but the rest of the band was taken away without further incident.

In Auglaize County the Shawnees had a large reservation, upwards of 100,000 acres, in and around present-day Wapakoneta, land the United States very much wanted. A Quaker mission there was headed by Henry Harvey who grew very fond of the tribe and who later wrote a book on Shawnee history and of his relationship with them. He was present during treaty negotiations in 1831 and thought that the treaty the government negotiated was so flawed it represented a fraud. He traveled to Washington with a group of Shawnees to complain and there they won some concessions. But a year later it was time to go.

In September, 1832 he watched as a sorrowful group of Shawnees passed by the mission for the last time, headed for new lands in Missouri. "It was sorrowful to see those poor souls as they were leaving their homes and native land to seek another they knew nothing about as they cast their last look at their favored spot–at old Wapaughkonnetta," Harvey wrote. "They lamented most for having to leave the graves of fathers, mothers, brothers, sisters, and children to the mercy of a people who, while living cared little for them, and would care less for their dead."

He continued. "In their journey they passed by our Mission; all called and took their last farewell and many of them wept bitterly as they left us, and in despair would declare that they considered they were an undone people; that their land was gone; their homes and all they had to support their families on gone; that the winter would overtake them before they could reach their new homes and they feared their women and children would perish..."

After the Shawnees were gone Henry Harvey visited them three times in their far away homes, the last time in 1842. He witnessed their suffering and helped as much as he could, and his relationship with them deepened. "My object in penning these accounts is, that those who may read them, may see what the "Savages" as they are so wrongfully denominated, are when treated as human beings...I have been acquainted with many Indian tribes and I believe that if ever our race was used as they have been, we would be more vindictive–more savage by far than they."

One of the largest assemblages of Natives, and ultimately the last to leave Ohio, were the Wyandots in present-day Wyandot County. They lived on a sizable reservation in what is now the city of Upper Sandusky. A Methodist Mission had been established there in 1821 and a number of Natives had converted to Christianity.

The Wyandots resisted pressure by the United States to go, finally yielding in March, 1842. By then their reservation was surrounded by the plowed fields of settlers. Over the next year preparations were made to leave and numerous tribal councils were held as well as services in the Methodist Mission Church. The Wyandots also brought their dead from other parts of the reservation and reburied them in the mission cemetery.

In July, 1843 over 700 Wyandots gathered to leave and a large farewell ceremony attended by them and area whites was held at the Mission Church. Squire Grey Eyes, a tribal chief and ordained Methodist minister, addressed his people. "He exhorted them to be good Christians and to meet him in heaven.

In a most sublime and pathetic manner he discoursed upon all the familiar objects of a home—no longer theirs. He bade adieu to the Sandusky on whose waters they had paddled their light bark canoes and in whose pools they had fished, laved [bathed] and sported. He saluted in his farewell the forest and the plains of the Sandusky where he and his ancestors had hunted, roved and dwelled for many generations."

Under a broiling sun, the Wyandots left, their caravan of wagons stretching for miles. They reached Cincinnati a week later where riverboats would float them down the Ohio and Mississippi rivers then up the Missouri to their new homes in Kansas. As they boarded the boats, "they seem to linger and turn to the north as if to bid a last farewell to the tombs which they had deposited the remains of their deceased children and in which the bones of their fathers had been accumulating and moulding for untold ages."

The last organized Indian tribe in the state was now gone. The ethnic cleansing of Ohio had been completed.

*The Methodist Mission in Upper Sandusky is where many of the Wynadots gathered before going west in 1843, the last tribe to leave Ohio.*

# CHAPTER IV

VOICES FROM THE BLACK SWAMP

*From New York to Wood County*

In December, 1836, Thomas Tracy left upstate New York alone in a one-horse wagon, $800 in gold under the front seat. His destination some 700 miles away was Wood County. There he purchased 80 acres on a sand ridge along what is now West Wooster Street in the city of Bowling Green and returned to New York for his family.

On May 2, 1837 Mr. Tracy gathered his clan for the last time in "the large room that had served for many years as kitchen, dining room, sitting room, and place for public worship." There they said a prayer and "with dimmed eyes" left behind their home of 42 years for new lives in a new land. One of his sons, J. R. Tracy, later recorded his experiences of traveling to and settling in the Black Swamp.

The journey from New York was uneventful until they reached Fremont, then Lower Sandusky, and "were about to plunge into the much talked of and greatly dreaded Black Swamp. We had heard much about it, of its thirty-two taverns in the thirty-one miles from Lower Sandusky to Perrysburg [the Maumee and Western Reserve Road], of families lodged three nights in the same house, meanwhile struggling hard each day to make a scant half-mile of progress through the bottomless mud..."

The Tracy's own close encounter with a mudhole did not take long. Eight miles west of Lower Sandusky stood two wag-

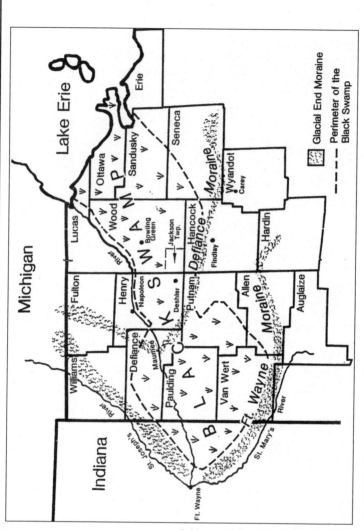

© *Maumee Valley Historical Society 1984*

*The Great Black Swamp covered all or part of 12 counties in Ohio as well as part of Indiana. (Map courtesy of Lucas County/Maumee Valley Historical Society).*

ons completely stalled. One, a group of Germans, were in the process of unloading their mired vehicle and muttering away in their native tongue. They had laid logs across the mud large enough to bear the weight of a person. "Upon this bridge a buxom lass would walk and steady the heavy box or bundle on the head of some man while he struggled shoreward" and out of the mud, Tracy wrote.

The other group at this mudhole had given up after only one day and were headed back to Lower Sandusky to take the Sandusky River to Lake Erie then around to Perrysburg. They encouraged the Tracys to do the same, but they continued on, preferring to fight the mud than trust the "awful waves" of Lake Erie. After a struggle the Tracy clan slogged past the mudhole and stopped for the night.

The next morning they came across a particularly deep hole where "one horse of my team fell and went so completely under that only the top of his head and a strip along his back was visible," Tracy recalled. They pulled through that stretch and made it to Woodville around midday. There they left the Maumee and Western Reserve Road, traveling now on a trail along the Portage River to Forks of Portage, now Pemberville, where they spent the night. They made fairly good progress the next day until it was time to leave the Portage River trail and head due west across open marsh toward the sand ridges that were destined to become the city of Bowling Green.

There they encountered a "veritable lake," Tracy recalled. "The water was about a foot deep and the grass, now the twenty-third of May, about a foot out of the water...a sea of living, moving green, beautifully undulating in the light breeze, glistening in the sunlight and always indicating that just a few rods ahead we should reach solid ground; an illusion that held good the entire distance to the foot of the ridges."

Once there the New York natives realized what they had gotten themselves into. "We very soon discovered that the condition in which we found the east prairie was not exceptional...mud ruled everywhere. Indeed, we found that the "Black Swamp" was not just a narrow strip on either side of the Western Reserve Pike but a vast area...." They also learned they had entered the kingdom of the mosquito. "No night was too dark or precinct too sacred for them to get in their work," Tracy recalled. "Like the frogs of Egypt they invaded every part of our dwelling but unlike the frogs, unless crushed, they refused to die."

Only the smoke of the smudge pot provided any real relief. "Many a meal was eaten with a smudge under the table and many a would be sleeper owed what rest he secured to the smoke that overspread his bed and compelled his bloodthirsty assailants to retire." Horse flies, the size of bees, took their toll as well, often leaving the poor horses streaked with blood.

There were other things young Tracy quickly learned about his new home. Shortly after he arrived he was digging a hole and reached down into it to pull out a root, or so he thought. "When my hand came fairly in sight you may judge of my disgust, or horror, or consternation upon discovering a snake, many times larger than I had ever before seen, in my clutch

© Metroparks 1988

*The water and mud of the Great Black Swamp were major impediments to the settlers traveling through it. From the Great Black Swamp display, Packer-Hammersmith Center, Pearson Metropark, Oregon. (Courtesy Toledo Area Metroparks).*

and notwithstanding I had some two feet of her double in view, neither end was in sight."

Tracy immediately let go but his dog Trip, a veteran snake killer, would have none of that. "Meanwhile, Trip had been intently watching, possibly suspecting I would be making some such fool move, saw my blunder and almost before the snake was out of my grasp, he had her in his. There was no squeamishness manifested now. A few energetic jerks and he had her in the open"

"He tried now to kill her," Tracy continued, "as he kills garter snakes, by shaking her to bits but he did little more than wiggle his own body while she seemed intent upon getting him within her coil. More than once he had to break his hold and jump to escape her."

A day or two later, in the same clearing, came another snake encounter, except this one Trip gave a wide berth to. "I saw a small brown snake, neatly coiled, with her head about six inches above the coil and giving forth an ominous rattling that told to a certainty the character of our find," Tracy wrote. " A smart blow from the club dispatched her."

"Now here is a question," Tracy wondered. "How did that dog know that he might attack the big racer with impunity, but must fight shy of the stroke of that small rattler? I am quite sure these two were the first of their kind he had ever seen." How did Trip know  "absolutely which he might attack and which he must avoid? Who can tell?

Tracy gives no clue as to why he cast snakes in the female gender.

Like virtually every other Black Swamp settler, Tracy experienced the terrible fever and violent tremors of swamp fever, or ague. "I want to tell you if there is anything in the world that will stay by a fellow when it has found him it is the ague," Tracy wrote. "My! How it will snuggle up to him, and hug him, and squeeze him, and shake him, and freeze him, and then bake him and fry him, until it would seem every drop of moisture is out of him..."

Tracy then talked about the cruelest part of the disease where the symptoms would stop for a day or two, only to return with a vengeance. "Then upon leavetaking [the ague] will soothingly whisper, 'don't get lonesome, will be back tomorrow, or next day, or worst of all, in three days.' Pitiable indeed was the state of one doomed to a three days waiting. Besides the long continuance of the dread of it, he knew, or soon learned that nothing was escaped by the delay. The energy of the performance was sure to be doubled, or trebled as the case might be, without discount."

"And so the round went on," Tracy continued. "Week by week, month by month, sometimes year by year (Brother Isaac was held two years, didn't go to school or do a day's work in that time) until as the phrase went the 'ague was worn out' and quit of sheer exhaustion."

J. R. Tracy wraps up his Black Swamp memoir thus: "Does the reader ask, have you not somewhat overdrawn the matter in this yarn you have spun us? In sober truth I think I have not. Did you leave the country? No, we did not. Will you pray tell us what you found that could induce anyone to stay? Perhaps, but not in this story."

### The Cruel Winter

The fall of 1842 was a mild one according to historical accounts, that lazy, delicious weather known as Indian Summer lasting late into November. The Black Swamp settlers may have been lulled into a bit of complacency for what followed may have been the worst winter of that century.

On the afternoon of November 25th the sky turned leaden and a cold rain began to fall. It soon became a wind-driven sleet and by morning, snow. In the weeks that followed the snow kept falling and the temperature bottomed out, eventually freezing the Maumee River to its bed.

In the dark months that followed there was little relief and when April began, there was still enough snow and ice on the ground to pull a sleigh. In early April, 1843 a Wood County pioneer named Amos Dewese encountered a fellow settler named Jonathan Stull. He was carrying a sack of corn and suffering mightily from the brutal winter.

"Stull was much depressed and discouraged on account of the terrible hard winter," Dewese wrote. "We talked of Adventism, as the Millerites said the end of the world was at hand.

Mr. Stull said he prayed for it every day, as he had seen all the trouble he wanted to see."

"He said he had eight head of horses and all had died; twenty-eight head of cattle and 260 head of hogs, and all were dead...He told me that he had been married twelve years; they had ten children, all of whom were almost nude. Not one of them had a full suit. They hadn't a bed or a window in the house."

The desperate Mr. Stull went on to say, "I have one peck of ears of corn in this sack and when I take it home and grind it in the hand-mill and mix it with water, bake and eat it with my wife and ten children, God knows where the next will come from. They must starve." The dam holding back Mr. Stull's emotions then gave way as his face crumpled and "he wept like a child."

The harsh winter had taken a toll on other Black Swamp settlers as well. In traveling about Wood County, Amos Dewese wrote that he passed "a number of cabins, forsaken and uninhabited. They looked gloomy enough, surrounded by ice and water and the dismal swamp. One of which had belonged to a John Ford which was new. A number of wild hogs had taken possession. They had piled on top of each other and there perished with cold and hunger."

During that cruel winter thousands of domestic and wild animals perished and the ones that survived were mere skeletons. It was a "terrible winter," according to Dewese, "never to be forgotten by the old settlers. Many had to move out of the Black Swamp before spring."

*First Generation Settler*

Samuel Skinner was 16 years old when he came with his parents and four brothers and sisters to the Great Black Swamp in 1830, then a virtually untouched wilderness. Part of the first wave of settlers in the area that changed the land forever, they settled in Washington Township in Sandusky County, which was near the eastern edge of the Swamp.

September, 1893 found Samuel Skinner to be an old man and living in Fremont. He began writing down some recollections of his younger days, thoughts tinged with sadness and regret of a life of toil and hardship. He began, "I have often thought of writing something of my life for my children to read when I am gone which will not be very long anymore. Soon will be 80 years old."

"I was born in Perry County, Ohio May 10, 1814 Came to this county April 10, 1830...It was truly a black swamp then, there was but three families then living in Washington township when we settled in it. Not one laid-out road in it. I help cut the first one, which was the Rollersville Road" [now US 6].

"It did seem to me I could not stay here," Skinner wrote. "Could see nobody, nothing but the big woods and wild animals–they was very plenty ...If I had a little money I certainly would not staid here. Should have run away from my father's home. But having no money kept me here." In 1831 Skinner's mother died and his father remarried, which added two more children to the crowded household. "That made it worse if possible," Skinner recalled.

In 1833 Skinner was married and he and his young wife Elizabeth built a log cabin on a heavily-wooded 80-acre lot over a span of ten days. "The house was 16x18 clapboard. Roof held down by waited poles," Skinner recalled. "Board holes in the wall and put poles in for bedstead...Don't think there was

*Samuel Skinner saw the Great Black Swamp transformed from its original state to cities, towns, and farms.*

1/2 pound of nails used in house. Cut a hole in walls, tacked strips across and pasted grease paper on it for window. We had no chairs in the house for 2 years. Used stools made out of split basswood. No saw mills; could not get lumber if we even had the money."

"It was a very wet lot, at times it was near all under water. When we began to keep house we was very poor indeed. I think if everything we had would not brought 50 dollars." Skinner and his wife "went to work was both of us well and hearty. Cleared off a patch that winter for corn and potatoes. In the spring planted it. Growed nice until the June flood came. Everything drowned out. We saw hard times indeed."

"We often had no bread for days at a time, " Skinner continued. "We sifted bran and made bread of that. At times lived on corn bread and wild meat mostly." The woods and marsh of the Black Swamp were rich in game then. "The wild animals were deer, turkey, wolves, wild cat, coon, opossum, and porcupine. Many a night I got up and shot off the gun to drive the wolves away. But never killed one."

Skinner had to supplement his income working at a mill on the Portage River six miles away. "Got 50 cents per day, he wrote. "Got one bushel of corn for one day's work. We used corn bread mostly."

Soon the Skinner family began to grow. "The next July, Wash was born [George Washington Skinner]. Then we had something to amuse ourselves with. Our family increased fast. Soon had a family of ten children [Wash and nine daughters] and it makes my heart ache to think back how they was raised compared to the way children are raised now. They went barefoot 8 months in the year and clothes very scanty indeed."

A life of toil was the only thing Skinner and his wife Elizabeth knew. "You may think that strange to look at things as they are now," he reminisced. "But it seemed all rite, we did not no anny better. We worked with a will." Given the opportunity, and with the benefit of hindsight, would he have again carved a life out of the Black Swamp wilderness? "Knowing what I do now and was young again I would not take a section of land there as a gift and go through the same hardships."

In May, 1894 Skinner wrote about an 1842 murder trial in

which he served as a juror. "About 50 years ago I was on a jury to try Mr. Sperry for murdering his wife. It commenced Monday morning. Saturday at noon we got the charge from the judge. We stood 6 to 6 [vote] till Sunday about 9 o'clock we called the judge to give this charge over on certain points. Went back to our room and soon agreed; found him guilty of murder in the first degree. All circumstantial evidence. Mr. Rose and I were the last to agree to it. He was sentenced to be hung on Sunday."

He continued. "Before he was to hang his children was brought in to see him. He managed to get a small pocket knife of his little boy. After they left he opened the large vessel in his arm and bled to death. That was the last of him. Well, now I am the only one living that had anything to do with the trial."

In October, 1898 Skinner wrote "65 years ago today I was married for the first time. Don't seem half that long...I dreamed the other night I was going south east to our old cabin. There was Jane [a daughter] trying to clear a patch for corn. Those things trouble me to think how you children was raised compared to the way they are now."

Three years later, his health failing and wishing he saw his children more often, he made his final entry. "Since writing the above have suffered with terrible kidney trouble...I learned our President died last night [President McKinley assassinated]. I feel that I must soon follow and leave all things here. Solom thought, I wish I could see all once more. Try and prepare for the end."

Samuel Skinner, who saw the Black Swamp in Sandusky County transformed from wilderness to towns and farms, died in 1902 and was buried in Fremont.

### Black Swamp Spuds and Snakes

Noah Prowant was born in Perry Township, Putnam County in 1864 in what was then the southwestern part of the Black Swamp. His family first came to the area in 1836 and the Swamp had been somewhat tamed by the time Noah came along.

One of his childhood recollections was being hired by farmers to dig potatoes growing in the rich soils of recently drained land. "We boys would frequently go to the prairie in the fall to dig potatoes," he wrote. "It was called a prairie but in reality was not a prairie rather a marsh."

"The writer would frequently dig 50 bushels in a day receiving 1.00," Prowant continued. "At this time it seem to not be much of a wage but the 1.00 seemed to have more value than now as one could purchase more with it." Some of the things he bought included school books and clothes, and money to go to the county fair.

"While working in the marsh were all ways on the watch lest we be bit by rattle snakes, none of our bunch were ever bitten but some working there would frequently hear of it hap-

*This undated photo of the Hardesty family of Paulding County is how typical Black Swamp settler family looked. Inscribed in hand on the back is, "Picture was taken out of bonfire on the day of the estate sale of Mrs. Ida Hardesty by Mrs. Edith Pritchard, M.D.--Paulding." (Ida Hardesty Family Portrait courtesy of the Center for Archival Collections, Bowling Green State University).*

pening," Prowant wrote. "On this marsh the popular remedy for the bite was whiskey. One of these fellows working nearly all the time in the marsh said he was so saturated with whiskey that when he was bitten by a snake it did not seem to hurt him but the snake keeled over and died (possibly this should be taken with a grain of salt)."

The advent of modern methods of mowing contributed to the demise of the Black Swamp rattlesnake. "The mowing machine is death to snakes," Prowant wrote. "The rattle snake fears nothing when the mowing machine approaches [the] snake coils with head erect ready to strike but when machine approaches there is nothing for him to strike and he loose his head."

Hogs were another method of snake control. "Most farmers keep hogs and hogs are destructive to snakes. When they discover a snake will make a noise as they do when wanting to gang up on something," Prowant wrote. "One will approach the snake presenting his jaw to the snake. The snake will strike at that instant, the hog will grab him as will the other hogs. They tear it [to] pieces and eat it."

Great flocks of carrier pigeons, now extinct, once darkened the skies in this country and childhood tales told to Noah Prowant give an insight into their demise. "I have been told by the older people they would sometimes go to the brushy edges of these parts in the night with a lantern and a club and take wild pigeons that were roosting in these brush. The lantern seemed to blind them, they would not fly away. These hunters would apply their club [and] knock them off there perch [and] gather them and put in a sack. Often did not use a club but gather them up as one can take chickens off their perches. These methods and probably other elements of destruction has caused the extinction of this beautiful bird and none has been seen for years."

# CHAPTER V

DRAINING THE BLACK SWAMP

For thousands of years the Great Black Swamp existed, remnants of a once vast glacial lake. As the millennia passed it lay undisturbed, known only to the wildlife that lived in it and the aboriginal peoples who occasionally hunted it. When the 1800's dawned it was still a pristine wilderness of towering trees, marshy meadows, and wild animals, a domain incompatible with human existence at the time.

But changes were looming, big changes, as new people were streaming to the land. At first they went no further than the edge of the great marsh and, peering in and seeing its rich, dark soil, inky waters and cathedral stands of trees that turned daylight into dark, named it the Black Swamp. Home also to deep water and mud that could sink a horse to its chest in the spring, ravenous clouds of mosquitoes in the summer, and malarial fevers in the fall, its perimeter was penetrated by few.

Even as lands around and beyond the Black Swamp were being devoured as the 19th century progressed, the Swamp remained above it all, so to speak. For several decades it remained an island that pioneers detoured around, sort of a forbidden forest. What few settlers were there lived in cabins clinging to riverbanks or on the occasional sand ridges that rose from the Swamp's flatness.

As late as 1840 the Black Swamp was still holding its own, the majority of the land within it averaging less than five persons per square mile with most of those square miles uninhabited and untouched. But with most of the tillable land available for settlement east of the Mississippi taken, settlers set their sights on the Swamp. In the next 60 years the Great Black Swamp, which had existed many thousands of years, would essentially disappear.

The forests of the Swamp were a major impediment and cutting down the trees and clearing the stumps was slow, backbreaking work. But with time and sweat a lot could be cleared. The major challenge to the settler was what to do with all that water. The power of the Swamp lay in its moisture, for it was water that prevented travel, bred mosquitoes and malaria, and nourished wild growth. For the settlers to beat the Swamp they had to take away its power by draining it .

The Maumee and Western Reserve Road running from Fre-

*These stumps in a Paulding County field give an idea of the thickness of the forest in the Black Swamp. Paulding County was one of two counties entirely within the confines of the Swamp, the other being Wood. (Photo courtesy of the Center for Archival Collections, Bowling Green State University.)*

mont to Perrysburg in the northern part of the Swamp had been, since its inception around 1811, a notorious 30-mile mudhole. However a major upgrade of the road in 1838-39 had demonstrated that high, dry land could be created if drainage ditches leading to area streams were dug deep enough. This was a bit of a revelation to the settlers as the majority of them were from the more hilly areas of the eastern United States or countries of Europe and had no experience in draining the land.

Early efforts at surface drainage were crude and haphazard. Often times a farmer would dig a nice, sloping ditch that did a fine job of ridding his land of excess water. The problem was that it sometimes ended up on the property of his neighbor, which led to more than a few lively discussions. As time went on it was obvious that an organized and systematic strategy was needed if the Swamp was to be drained.

Prompted by this need and the cholera outbreaks of the 1850's, which was frequently spread through contaminated water, the first in a series of "ditch laws" in Ohio was passed in 1859. These gave county officials the right to enter and, if necessary, seize land for the purpose of ditch projects that were in the public interest. One of the more dramatic examples of the ditching that drained the Swamp can be found in southwestern Wood County where flows what appears to be a natural river with deep, tree-lined banks. This body of water is actually the Jackson Cut Off, a nine mile ditch dug in the late 1870's that drains parts of Wood, Henry, Putnam and Hancock counties.

The Black Swamp farmer also soon learned that removing the surface water was not enough. Underdrainage to remove excess water below the surface of the soil of the former marsh was needed for maximum crop output. The first underdrains were crude, often consisting of saplings or stones laid in a trench and covered over, drains which deteriorated rather quickly. A longer lasting method was developed which was to nail two planks together into the shape of a "V" which was laid inverted in a trench and covered.

By far the best method of underdrainage would prove to be clay tile but there were no tile factories anywhere near northwest Ohio and the cost of freighting them in was well beyond the means of most farmers. Then in the 1860's it was realized that underneath the rich topsoil of the Swamp lay a tremendous bed of clay and by 1880 scores of clay tile factories had sprung up in the Black Swamp counties. The access to drainage tile fully unlocked the rich soils of the Swamp and farmers there were quicker to show a profit than those who settled in drier areas of the state, who frequently took a generation or more before they were in the black.

In the next twenty years settlement reached a climax, and when the century closed, little evidence remained of the vast, slumbering wetland that once covered much of northwest Ohio. Ironically, it was the forests of the Swamp that provided the wood for the early underdrains and later, fuel to fire the tile kilns. The clay subsoil provided the raw material for abundant and cheap drainage tile. In the end, the elements that made up the Swamp were crucial in its elimination.

*This "river" as seen from Milton Center in Wood County is actually the Jackson Cut Off, a major drainage ditch that drains parts of four Black Swamp counties.*

# CHAPTER VI

INDIAN SUNSET

*Author's Note: The following is the first of several stories containing selections from the Dresden Howard Papers. Colonel Dresden Howard was an early Maumee Valley pioneer who was known for his friendship with area Indians. A story on his life was told in The Great Black Swamp.*

The year was 1850 and the Maumee Valley had undergone tremendous change in the previous five decades. When the century started, thousands of Indians still roamed the valley as the mass of settlers and government removal policy that would sweep the Indians from the valley were still a few years down the road.

However fifty years later they were virtually gone. So were the tribal villages and fields of corn, squash, pumpkins and beans that once lined the banks of the Maumee. One Native family that remained was that of Teenabeek and his wife and three young children of the Ottawa tribe. Said by Dresden Howard to be the last full-blooded Natives of any tribe in the region, they lived in the woods outside of the riverside village of Grand Rapids, Ohio, then called Gilead. Teenabeek was able to eke out a living hunting and trapping while his wife dressed animal skins and made sugar in the spring. She also made baskets, moccasins and toys to trade with the whites for food and clothing.

Howard's experience with, and attitude toward, Indians was vastly different than those of most Americans, especially those on the frontier. Growing up in Gilead, he spent his childhood playing with Indian children and became fluent in a number of Native dialects. As a youth and a young man he was welcome at any Native campfire in the area and never viewed Indians in an adversarial or hostile light.

He enjoyed visiting Teenabeek and his family in their camp where they often talked about the old days. They also talked about the days to come, when Teenabeek would be forced to leave. "I was in the habit of occasionally spending an evening in his camp and rehearsing old times with my friend," Howard wrote. "He well understood the situation, that his people were rapidly passing away and the land that was theirs would know them no more."

One morning Teenabeek's wife came to Howard visibly upset. "I knew that some misfortune had befallen her," he wrote. "I asked her if the Great Spirit was angry and she answered 'yes,' that her husband was very sick and she wished me to come." Howard hurried to their camp and found Teenabeek with a high fever, his face terribly swollen from the bite of a poisonous spider. Despite a doctor's attention, he died a few days later.

"I went over early one morning to see them and found the poor squaw seated on the ground by her dead husband, her head bowed on her breast, her face as well as the children's painted black in token of mourning," Howard wrote. "There was no one now to hunt or trap and aid the destitute squaw to support the three helpless papooses. The eldest being a boy of nine years."

Howard asked her what she wanted to do with his body and without raising her head she said, "I have no home, my people are far away." With great sadness she spoke of how the "land of her fathers had been taken by the pale face, that his heart was small, that he would not give back to the red mother land enough to bury the body of the dead hunter."

Howard told her he could be buried in his family cemetery in Gilead, "on the banks of the Maumee, where the waters shall always at midnight sing the death song of the hunter who has gone on his last trail." She replied to him, "my brother has a big heart. The Great Spirit will be good to him."

Howard went to Gilead and had a grave dug and a coffin made. When he returned to the Indian camp the next morning with several others, "we found the squaw still setting as I had left her, her head still bowed in mourning and the children still setting in a corner of the lodge, nearly as still as their dead father. No one spoke or moved as we entered, until I spoke and told her we had come to take away the dead and bury it from sight."

She placed her husband's rifle, tomahawk, and knife in the coffin as was the tradition for the journey to the next world. However Howard convinced her to keep these things, that her son would soon be a hunter and would need them.

The group journeyed to Gilead and to the Howard Cemetery where Teenabeek was buried, the last full-blooded Indian to be buried in the Maumee Valley. Teenabeek's wife then took a seat at the head of his grave and burned some tobacco. There, she "watched the smoke rise to the clouds notifying the Great Spirit ( Manito) that a soul was on the way to the Spirit land." She remained at the grave until dark, returning several evenings in a row and repeating the same ceremony.

Now Teenabeek's grieving widow was confronted with a major dilemma. With the prospect of surviving on her own out of the question, she would have to leave and find her Ottawa tribe either on lands west of the Mississippi or on reservations in Canada. She came to Howard and told him she had made the decision to go to Canada and Mrs. Howard supplied her with pork and flour for the journey. "After thanking us the impressive way that only an Indian can [and saying] that the Great Manito would always be good to us, she slipped away and was seen no more."

Later that day as the light was waning, a birch bark canoe bobbed over the rapids of the Maumee River and past the village. In it was Teenabeek's wife, her three young children, and all her worldly possessions. With a heavy heart, Howard watched as this courageous woman faded into the dusk, leaving behind forever her homeland and the grave of her husband. And as the sun set over the land, so too had it set over

THE GREAT BLACK SWAMP II:

the Indians of the Maumee Valley. "I have no doubt that Teenabeek was the last [full-blooded] Indian buried on the banks of the Maumee," Howard wrote.

Dresden Howard also wrote that later generations standing where he stood that evening would little realize that, "the last Indian woman and her children passed the spot where they stand in the silent darkness of evening in the spring of 1850, widowed and alone, knowing she was leaving the land of her people, that she was looking for the last time upon the spot where the father of her children was buried, that her race was nearly extinguished, and the remnants of her tribe forbidden to return."

# CHAPTER VII

THE MAUMEE INDIAN MISSION

In the fall of 1822 when the Maumee Valley was still a virtual wilderness, a group of white travelers landed in the frontier settlement of Maumee. Unlike the other whites arriving at the time seeking land and riches, it was hearts, minds, and souls this group was after. For they were missionaries sent to educate and otherwise "civilize" the Indians of the area whose world was rapidly shrinking.

One of the missionaries was Reverend Isaac Van Tassel and his wife Lucia. They were part of the original group of 13 mission members sent to teach Indians English, Christianity, and the white ways of living. In 1872 Lucia Van Tassel wrote down her recollections of her missionary days.

They began their work in a 16 x 60 log mission house on the high bank of the Maumee River about eight miles downriver from present-day Grand Rapids. "The Indians were at first shy and distrustful," she wrote, "they could not believe that white people intended them any good. As they became acquainted, however, they were very friendly and never gave us any trouble by stealing or committing any depredation."

Mrs. Van Tassel would have preferred to reach out to the Native women of the valley in their own language, which she eventually learned in her spare time. "It would have been far more agreeable to my wishes to spend my time in studying the language and instructing adult native females than otherwise," she wrote. "But this was not the plan of our mission.

Our instructions were to collect all the native children we could into the school and teach them English. These had to be fed and clothed, consequently little could be done to elevate the adult natives."

Mr. Van Tassel and another missionary did travel to nearby Indian villages and preach to adults through an interpreter. "But the good which the missionaries had hoped to accomplish was often frustrated through the opposition of the Indian traders who made every effort to keep them intoxicated as much as possible," Mrs. Van Tassel wrote. 'To civilize and Christianize the Indians would be to deprive them of their unrighteous gains."

Life on the frontier was hard for just about everyone and the missionaries were no exception. Going into their second year, illness was rampant and they had exhausted their first year's supplies. "Nothing but corn could be procured and that, for want of a mill to grind it, had for some weeks, to be eaten whole. No vegetables could be obtained, no potatoes, not even for seed," Mrs. Van Tassel wrote. "We were told that 'potatoes would not grow on Maumee' but the third spring a vessel came into the river laden with potatoes. Mr. Van Tassel went down and bought 40 bushels and we never afterwards wanted for potatoes."

In November, 1823 an eight-year-old half Indian boy named Samuel, staying at the mission, was sent downriver on an errand. Night came and he did not return. His father was notified and a frantic search ensued of the Indian camps and woods of the Maumee Valley to no avail. The days turned into weeks and all hope was lost.

Then word was received that some Indians had found a boy in the woods and taken him to Findlay. "His father and a companion started immediately for that place and about twenty miles from the station met Samuel walking slowly, supporting himself with a stick in each hand," Mrs. Van Tassel wrote. "When asked where he was going he said he was going home to the station, that he had been lost in the woods a long time and had lived on nuts; but for two days had been in a swamp where he could find none and he was almost starved. Twenty-one days he had subsisted on nuts."

In 1826 the mission took in a young Indian left behind by his hunting party sick and unable to travel, his body wracked with tuberculosis. "While his strength lasted he was anxious to make himself useful and would cheerfully offer to do any little chores which he felt able to do, but he was soon confined to bed," Mrs. Van Tassel recalled. "We never carried him a dish of food or cup of cold water without receiving his emphatic wawanee, wawanee (thank you, thank you). He died apparently happy, trusting in the Savior."

By the end of 1826, nearly all the original missionaries had left, sickness and other hardships having taken their toll. However the Van Tassels remained and continued to operate the mission and the school which at times had as many as 50 children, although the average was around 30. "The children were

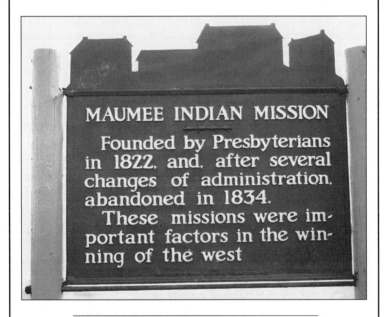

*This marker on State Route 65 between Waterville and Grand Rapids is the only evidence of the Indian Mission that once was there.*

generally docile and affectionate to their teachers and others, though from different tribes," Mrs. Van Tassel wrote. "Disturbances seldom occurred among them and they learned as fast as children in general."

However the number of Indians were dwindling due to the government removal policy. In 1834, the mission closed its doors for good. No trace of the Indian mission remains today, save for a roadside historical marker. The attitudes of the missionaries might be considered to be paternal if not condescending by today's standards. However at the time, exploitation and removal represented the dominant attitude of whites toward the Native-Americans of northwestern Ohio. For the missionaries to travel to, and live in, a hostile frontier environment toward a loftier and more compassionate goal was remarkable.

*A Student's Perspective*

Then as now, the schoolroom experience, as viewed by the student, diverges from that of the teacher, especially when youngsters would rather be out playing. One of the few white children in the mission school was Dresden Howard who later wrote about it. The Maumee Valley was a giant playground to him and his Indian friends. Then the school came along and young Dresden's father wanted him to get some of the three R's.

"We spent our time at the village in summer shooting bow and arrows, fishing or swimming in the river and in many other plays and sports peculiar to Indian boys and you can imagine that it was almost death to shut us away from these pastimes and shut up too, in a school room where the presiding genius was a sanctimonious old maid of the hard shell, stiff-back, Yankee persuasion, where long prayers were said morning and evening and not a smile or whisper allowed," Howard recalled.

He said that many Indian children dropped out after a day or two and "could never be caught or tempted back, and if I could have got away I think I should have followed their example. I would have gladly hid in any of the Indian villages, in which I had many friends and acquaintances, but the Indians were too honest and would not have kept me hid me from my mother and father. So I was obliged, like many of my Indian playmates, to bear the restraints of the Mission..."

One of the things Howard and his playmates liked about the mission was the food. "Our food was healthy and abundant, consisting of beef, pork and beans, corn bread, corn and meal mush and milk for supper, mush fried and eaten with maple syrup for breakfast, potatoes and other vegetables for dinner ( but no tea or coffee at any time) and seasoned with good old fashioned blessing and family worship every morning and evening...we fared finely, and with warm and comfortable beds to sleep in, we certainly had no fault to find with the management in that direction."

The efforts of the mission teachers to introduce the Bible to Native children was largely in vain, according to Howard. "They took education readily but religion, sparingly and doubtingly." The Indians had their own theology and concept of eternal reward and damnation, Howard explained. "The great punishment of the bad Indian is in never being able to cross the great river to the happy hunting grounds, and that he will be obliged to wander up and down its banks in sight of his friends on the other side enjoying the cool shade of its groves and the sparkling waters of its pure and limpid springs and brooks and the freedom to chase the deer and the elk at pleasure."

Howard wrote that when not giving instruction, the mission teachers were kind. "There was nothing in the way of kindness that they would not do for any of us, and when not on duty were very social and pleasant to be with...good souls they were, but I think with an entirely too stiff and sanctimonious a religion to train a set of wild Indian boys and girls. I know it was bad medicine for us."

Despite his characterization of it as bad medicine, Howard was later grateful for his three years of schooling there as it turned out to be the only formal education he received. As for the Native children, "it educated many hundreds of the youths of these tribes of whom many in after years in their new homes west of the Mississippi became good farmers and mechanics..."

Fifty years after the mission closed, Dresden Howard passed its former grounds. Converted to a farm, its buildings were gone and its orchards neglected. As he gazed upon it what struck him the most was the silence. "The old school house bell that rang out its peals over the river and forest that was wont to call together that band of half savage children to school and prayers is silent, the noisy half Indian, half French, and half English gabble of a hundred Indian boys and girls is no more heard, and the life and active busy scenes of the old Mission have long since passed, and in its place, the quiet stillness of a farm."

# CHAPTER VIII

## A Tough Hombre

In the early days of the nineteenth century when the Maumee Valley was still primarily a Native home there came a white man, Peter Navarre. Grandson of a French army officer who first came to the Detroit area in 1745, Navarre was born at Detroit around 1788 and in 1807 came to the mouth of the Maumee River with his brother Robert and built a cabin on the east side, one of the earliest whites to settle in the area. "Muskrat French," Peter Navarre and his brother were, the name given to those early trappers and traders for whom riverbanks and valleys were home.

As a young man he worked for a Detroit fur company and frequently traveled downriver to Fort Wayne to buy furs from the Indians. There he made friends with Little Turtle, the Miami chief. He knew many Natives and was fluent in the Potawatomi language as well as several other Native dialects.

In 1812 when war came to the valley, his knowledge of the terrain and of Indian language and ways made him valuable as a scout and a spy. He was under the command of General William Hull that year when Hull surrendered Detroit and all his forces to the British. Rather than surrender, Navarre reported to General William Henry Harrison for duty, a parole violation that led the British to place a $1,000 bounty on his head, a considerable sum of money in those days.

The following summer late in July he was with Harrison during the second siege of Fort Meigs. The British and their

Indian allies had been hammering away at the fort for several days with little success when the firing stopped on July 26th. Navarre learned that the British were to travel by boat to present-day Fremont and attack the lightly guarded Fort Stephenson and Harrison dispatched him with a message to the fort's commander to abandon his post and retreat.

With the note sewn in the collar of his shirt, Navarre left at sundown on the 29th in a raging thunderstorm for the dangerous 30-plus mile journey. Lying between him and his destination was the Great Black Swamp and Indians traveling by land toward the fort who were presumably well aware of the pile of money his head would bring.

It was, to say the least, a perilous journey, where any mis-

*This life-size painting of Peter Navarre, painted in 1867 when he was 80, hangs in the Local History and Genealogy Department of the Toledo-Lucas County Public Library.*

calculation, lapse in judgment, or noise, such as breaking a twig, could bring about certain death. Traveling all night and into the next day, he dodged Indians on several occasions and had to swim the Sandusky River twice to avoid detection, but he arrived at Fort Stephenson the afternoon of the 31st. By this time the British and Indians had the fort just about surrounded, so it's not clear if Navarre ever actually delivered the message. He did however return to Fort Meigs and update Harrison on the situation.

Harrison was quite grateful to have such a daring scout working for him and put him right back to work. In August he delivered a message to Harrison from Commodore Perry at what is today Port Clinton that Perry needed more soldiers. Navarre then led a group of Kentucky sharpshooters back to Port Clinton to join Commodore Perry's forces.

On September 9th he delivered a message from Harrison to Perry telling him to attack the British fleet at once. Perry attacked the next day and the Battle of Lake Erie was won. The Kentucky sharpshooters played an important role as they picked off a number of British sailors from the decks of Perry's fleet. Historians believe it was Navarre who delivered Perry's legendary message of triumph back to Harrison, "we have met the enemy and they are ours."

On another occasion Navarre was traveling on a risky mission with an unknown companion when they stopped for the night. The companion wanted to build a fire to warm their supper, a request Navarre ignored. The companion went on to bother Navarre about a fire and also remarked about the number of owls he heard hooting in the forest. Finally Navarre lit a small fire then instructed the companion to follow him to a thicket where they concealed themselves. Soon a prowling Indian came into view. "There's your owl," Navarre grumbled. The subject of a fire did not come up again.

Another tale has Navarre leading a scouting party from Fort Meigs to investigate a report of an Indian war party which had crossed the ice of Lake Erie to attack settlers in the Maumee Valley. At one point he proceeded on alone, telling his men that if he did not return to go back to the fort. That night Navarre found the camp of the Indians, who had been drinking, slipped past the drowsy picket guards, and reached the sleeping body of warriors.

There he took the ramrod of his gun and left a message in Indian characters in the snow and sprinkled gunpowder over it. He then returned to his men and then to the fort. The next morning the Indians awoke, saw the friendly warning, and thought the better of their plans and returned to Canada.

After the War of 1812 Navarre lived a generally quiet life, living all his years in East Toledo. He was known for his polite demeanor and had a large family. Five of his sons served in the Civil War. When William Henry Harrison returned to the Maumee Valley to campaign in the 1840 presidential election Peter Navarre was an honored guest. Because he was not officially a soldier in the American army he was ineligible for a pension. However in recognition of his service, Congress awarded him an eight dollar per month pension in 1864 along with a medal.

Peter Navarre lived ten more years before dying March 20, 1874 in East Toledo and was buried in an unmarked grave in Mount Carmel Cemetery. He served as president of the Maumee Valley Pioneer Association for a time before his death. Navarre Park in East Toledo was named after him as was Navarre Avenue, believed to have once been a trail he frequently used to travel between the river and woods.

A cabin built by one of his sons and one he probably stayed in as a guest stands in Toledo Botanical Garden where it has been restored to reflect early pioneer life. And a life size painting of him hangs in the local history department of the Toledo-Lucas County Library, a tough hombre.

# CHAPTER IX

## THE INDIAN ELM

It's been gone a long time now, but on Harrison Street in Maumee directly across the Maumee River from Fort Meigs once stood a massive tree, the Indian Elm. A favored gathering place of the Ottawa and Potawatomi of the Maumee Valley, it was also known as the Council Elm, the Maumee Elm, and even the Sniper's Elm.

Dresden Howard described it as "a white elm standing on a beautiful spot on the north bank of the river, being four or five feet in diameter and fifty feet to the first limb. It was crowned by an immense top that covered with its shade many square rods of beautiful greensward." In addition to the beauty of the tree's location, the air around it filled with the "never ceasing murmur" of the rapids that creased the river in front of Fort Meigs, according to Howard.

"This spot was an enchanting one, selected long ago by the Indians as a favorite Council Ground," Howard wrote. "Its cloud sweeping boughs had been perfumed with more of the incense of the sacred Council pipe than any tree in this valley. War and peace had been born under its branches. It was a cathedral, a Court House; it was to the Indian what the State House is to Ohio or West Minster Hall to London...Through the centuries it was a guide to the eagles and a landmark to the storms. In the heat of summer days the old Maumee, in its winding, weary journey to the unsalted seas, took after dinner naps in its cool shade."

The tree also witnessed the Maumee Valley's change from a Native population to a European one, and some of the events that led up to that change. On August 20, 1794 Indian warriors fleeing the Battle of Fallen Timbers passed beneath its branches heading for the safety of their Swan Creek camps.

In 1813 the tree saw the last attempt by the Indians of the area to throw off their white invaders. In May of that year during the first siege of Fort Meigs, an Indian sniper scaled the tree and fired through its foliage on the fort's soldiers creeping to the river's edge for water, killing one and wounding several others. Finally an American sharpshooter located him by the smoke of his rifle and a well-aimed bullet sent his body tumbling to the earth, a remarkable shot of about one half mile. The tree also witnessed the second siege in July that, like the first, ended with a British and Indian withdrawal.

During both sieges it's quite possible that the legendary Shawnee Chief Tecumseh stood beneath the tree, his thoughts troubled. There from the protection of its great trunk he watched the Americans across the river, his enemy he so passionately wanted to defeat, but deep in his heart he knew they would probably destroy him, as they did a few months later.

Over the next two decades the tree saw the valley below it change. The people that had called it home since time immemorial were leaving. In their place came new ones with a different color skin and a different language.

And in 1833, with the end of the existence of Indians in the Maumee Valley rapidly approaching, the last Indian Council was held under its boughs. This was a treaty meeting between the remaining Ottawas of the area and government treaty commissioners, and one in which a teen-aged Dresden Howard served as an interpreter. While the meeting was a peaceful one, it represented another in a line of defeats for the Maumee Valley Indians that began in 1794 at Fallen Timbers.

"This was the last gathering under the Old Council Elm," Howard wrote. "What a change from the Indian Chiefs with all the glitter and show of painted and silver trinkets, the bright and shining tomahawk pipes throwing off incense from the fragrant Kinnekenick, to the [present-day] lazy fisherman and canalmen in their dirty blankets smoking a short clay pipe filled with cheap tobacco."

The tree lived for nearly another 100 years before it died and was cut down in 1924. A small white stone on Harrison Street near Cass Street in Maumee marks the spot where this mighty elm once stood.

*The Indian Elm as it appeared late in its life. The memorial shaft at Fort Meigs, which was erected in 1908, can barely be seen in the distance across the Maumee River. The tree was removed in 1924. (Photo courtesy of the Local History and Genealogy Department, Toledo-Lucas County Public Library).*

# CHAPTER X

## MARCH TO FORT MEIGS

It was February of 1813 and the six month commitments of the current Ohio Militia were about to expire when Governor Meigs ordered a draft. The year 1813 would prove to be a climactic one in northwest Ohio as war raged again between the United States of America and England, and the two powers were destined to clash on the banks of the Maumee River at Fort Meigs.

One of the men drafted was Alexander Bourne of Chillicothe who wrote an account of what would be an interesting six months of his life. He was the 17th man taken and was notified on a Sunday evening to report on Monday morning. He quickly moved up to number three when the first 14 taken ran and hid in the woods.

Bourne's father had fought in the Revolution and he had no intention of shirking his duty. His friends encouraged him to hire a substitute, a common practice then. But he refused, even when a man offered to do his entire six months for $90.

He reported as ordered in Chillicothe and was appointed first sergeant, as the man who was supposed to serve in that capacity was missing, "having been drunk for about 14 years," according to Bourne. The sodden first sergeant eventually showed and Bourne then was given the rank of colonel and appointed adjutant to the colonel in command, Mills Stephenson, who had no uniform and who was "awkward & sheepish & appeared to know nothing about military duty."

When the regiment was about to march, Governor Meigs showed up for inspection and was so unimpressed with Colonel Stephenson that he ordered Colonel Bourne to assume command. The regiment marched and Stephenson "slunk back towards the rear of the column with the meekness of a sheep & all of us were ashamed of him." After about five miles of this, Bourne gave Stephenson back his command, apparently to put an end to his sideshow.

The regiment reached what is now Upper Sandusky where they camped for several days, the snow nine inches deep on the ground, and Bourne having but one blanket. They built a small stockade there, left a small company behind, and marched on ten miles. The next day Bourne was sent back to the stockade on some business in a cold rain that turned to heavy snow and nearly froze to death. But he survived and eventually rejoined the regiment.

His next mission was to scout the country that lay between the regiment and Fort Findlay, now Findlay, Ohio, and mark out a road to the fort. He left with three soldiers and four Indian guides and by the third day had reached the north bank of the Blanchard River. From there they continued downriver and saw the fort on the other side. But with the gates wide open, something was obviously wrong.

"I hailed as loud as I could but received no answer," Bourne wrote. He sent two Indians across on a raft and they confirmed that the fort had been deserted. Bourne and the rest followed and found that the fort was well stocked with arms and other supplies destined to be shipped to Fort Meigs later in the spring. The next day Bourne ordered one man to stay with him and the rest to return to the regiment and report their findings to Colonel Stephenson.

Bourne was now in a unique position. He found himself in charge of a frontier fort in hostile territory with thousands of dollars in government property and commanding an army of one: "the more danger the more honor," he wrote. Fearing an Indian attack, Bourne and his soldier secured themselves in a blockhouse and opened up a crate of muskets. They loaded 50 of them and lined them up against the blockhouse walls. But no Indians came and Bourne and his compatriot collected sap from nearby maple trees and made sugar to pass the time.

Several days later a captain and thirty men arrived, much to the relief of Bourne and his one-man army. Soon the rest of the regiment arrived and, leaving one company behind to garrison the fort, marched north for Fort Meigs. It was March and the weather was still cold.

"We had to cross a large tract of flat, wet land nearly all covered with water and ice in the winter called the Black Swamp," Bourne wrote. "I was well mounted but the Sergeant Major was sick & I let him ride my horse in the worst places & waded through myself, sometimes more than three feet deep– my health was good & I suffered no damage to it–but many of the soldiers were laid up with fevers, rheumatisms & colds. At length we arrived at Fort Meigs, the advanced post held by the North Western Army."

Fort Meigs was still under construction and troops were still arriving. Soon General William Henry Harrison arrived and "looked at our Col. Stephenson–conversed with him a few moments & then sent him off to command the port of Lower Sandusky which was only a Captain's command," Bourne wrote.

By mid-April the fort was fully garrisoned and preparing for an expected attack by the British. "The General ordered the Officers to drill their men every day & prepare them for actual service in the face of the enemy but very few of the officers had even seen a battle or knew anything about strict discipline, & needed drilling about as much as their men," Bourne lamented.

By the end of April, a formidable British and Indian army had massed across from Fort Meigs on the opposite side of the Maumee River. On May 1st an intense British bombardment was underway and "a constant stream of 24 pound balls & 10 inch bomb shells...we soon had a few men killed and wounded & some mangled in a shocking manner which was very revolting to my feelings at first but I soon become accustomed to it."

During the height of the shelling Bourne marched a small column of men in a manner that exposed them to fire and General Harrison let him know in no uncertain and very profane terms his disapproval of his tactics. Bourne was furious over being insulted in front of his own men and other officers. "My first impulse was to throw down my sword at his feet & let him arrest me forth with but the next moment I thought of a better way & saying nothing to him I sheathed my sword & marched deliberately over the same ground."

Bourne spent the rest of the day and the night expecting to be arrested. The next morning he saw General Harrison and an aide walking toward his blockhouse and was surprised that the General would come to arrest him in person. Instead Harrison said, "good morning adjutant," to which Bourne replied, "good morning general, I hope you are very well." Harrison then handed Bourne his personal telescope and asked him to observe a possible new British cannon site. Nothing more was said about the incident.

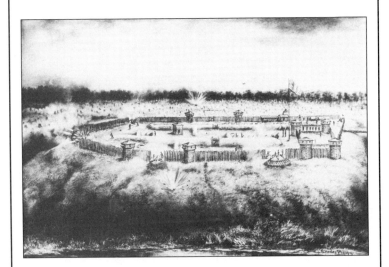

*This artist's conception of Fort Meigs was done on its 100th anniversary in 1913. While it does contain some inaccuracies, it does give an idea of what the fort might have looked like under fire.*

The intense bombardment continued and the fort's chief engineer Captain Eleazor Wood, for whom Wood County is named, ordered Bourne to have his men dig an entrenchment in front of his blockhouse on very exposed ground. The British were now firing red hot cannon balls in an attempt to blow up the fort's ammunition, balls that hissed and boiled in the ground, and more protection of the fort's wall was needed. The men were, of course, terrified.

"I informed Captain Wood that the men could not be kept at work–he then gave me an unlimited order on the Commissary for whiskey & directed me to give it to them every half hour & make them drink until they were insensible to fear, but not too drunk to stand and work. He said, 'There is no other way-it must be done in extreme cases!'" Fortified with liquid courage the soldiers, staggering and swearing, went about their dangerous duties. "The men then kept at their work, reeling and cursing the British & their hot balls until their work was finished. There were none killed or badly wounded."

One morning during the siege a Sergeant Major who appeared "wholly insensible to fear" came out of his blockhouse to wash. Bourne saw a shell descending near him and ordered him to hit the dirt "but he would not muddy his clothes to save his life." When the shell landed in the ground about four feet from him he still would not lay down but only stooped a little. The shell then burst and he was thrown down and covered with mud. "He got up laughing & shaking himself & appeared to enjoy the sport," Bourne marveled.

May 5th was the last day of the siege as the British and Indians withdrew. "We passed through a terrible conflict which tried our souls & bodies," Bourne wrote. Of about 50 officers, Bourne was the 14th mentioned in Harrison's order thanking his officers for bravery and good conduct.

The weather warmed and illness spread through the fort and in June Bourne became quite ill and was given a furlough to go home to recover. He had no horse, having sold his soon after he reached the fort, but he negotiated with the quartermaster general for an old pack horse to ride. He soon left with a small detachment of officers and friendly Indians for Fort Amanda, south of present-day Lima.

The first day they saw hostile Indians watching them but were left alone. The second day Bourne's old horse began to lag and his fellow officers, two of whom had borrowed money from him and promised to stand by him, left him behind. One of the Indians offered to ride along with him and whip his horse and Bourne paid him a quarter per mile to do so. But soon the old horse refused to do more than walk and Bourne found himself alone in hostile territory under a setting sun.

He walked until dark, let the old horse loose, and fired his pistols in case his traveling party was near. Getting no response, "I reloaded my pistols, laid them by my side & with sword, tomhawk & knife." He then laid down on his one blanket for the night "trusting in Divine Providence for protection." The night was lit by thunder and lightening and Bourne leaned up against a tree and spent a long night waiting for dawn.

The next morning he trudged on, "sick, sad, hungry & weary" with only two ounces of bread to eat. He came to the Blanchard River where he found the Indians and "my scurvy brother officers having ridden on all night to get to a place of safety but the Indians would not march in the morning until they had dried their blankets according to their custom & this probably saved me."

Bourne obtained another pack horse to ride and made it to Fort Amanda and eventually down the Miami River to the Ohio River and home to Chillicothe, his abandonment by his fellow officers leaving a bitter taste in his mouth. Even though he was home, he was still sick and nearly broke. However another adventure awaited him.

A General McArthur there engaged him to escort his wife and daughter to the Upper Blue Lick Spring in Kentucky, giving him a horse and paying his expenses. It was believed the waters of the spring had healing powers and the general's wife and daughter were also in poor health. The spring was owned by an eccentric former major who had served in the Revolution and who believed he could heal by charms. When Mrs. McArthur complained of a toothache he "rubbed her tooth with a red string [and] went into the woods to find a particular dogwood tree standing in a particular position around which he must tie the string," Bourne wrote. "I laughed so much at the old lady that she became angry & she would not tell me whether the Major had cured her tooth ache or not."

The spring's water rose through a "hollow sycamore log called a 'gum' about three feet in diameter set in the ground– It was clear and copious–mineralized with salt & sulphur & nauseous to the smell and taste." To derive the healing benefit of the water, it had to be drank.

One morning they were informed that "a very large fat woman who was there just before we came had lifted up her clothes, got into the water & sat down in it–her big backside filling up the gum–& we had been drinking after her. Oh snakes, toads & dung worms, the upper blue lick was done over! You need not speak of it for fifty years!"

As the appeal of this particular spring had been seriously diminished, the group moved on to a resort at Lower Blue Lick Spring. There they spent a week before returning to Chillicothe, their health restored. It was now August and Colonel Bourne's six month term of service had expired. But "I was without money or business. My friend Hough the Auditor gave me something to do in his office & so I laid down the sword & took up the pen again."

Alexander Bourne didn't know it at the time but three years later in 1816 he would return to the Maumee Valley as a U.S. land agent along with two surveyors. There they platted a town that came to be called Perrysburg.

# CHAPTER XI

## The First Railroad

It was early in the summer of 1837 when a ship tied up at the Maumee River docks in the infant city of Toledo and unloaded a strange-looking contraption. Onlookers scratched their heads as they viewed what looked like a giant iron cylinder laying on its side with large metal wheels and a tall smokestack with ADRIAN No. 1 emblazoned on it. No one could recognize this thing as a steam locomotive because no one had ever seen one before unless they had recently arrived from the East Coast. The steam railroad had come to the west.

People were even more amazed when this machine belched smoke and steam and hissed and snorted as it pulled away from its station at Monroe and Water streets. And as the first steam railroad west of the Allegheny Mountains chugged into the countryside, dogs barked, horses reared, and children ran alongside. They had seen the horse-drawn rail cars of the railroad when it debuted the year before but, forward motion without horse, man, water, or wind power was something new.

Advertisements promised settlers heading west they would "save two days and the corresponding expense by taking this route in preference to the more lengthened, tedious and expensive route heretofore traveled." The ad came with the disclaimer, "all baggage at the risk of owners."

The Erie & Kalamazoo Railroad ran from Toledo to Adrian, Michigan with a stop in Sylvania along the way with a fare of 50 cents to Sylvania and $1.50 to Adrian. The passengers rode in a Gothic-looking car called the "Pleasure Car" with two lower compartments and an upper one with more luxurious seating with eight seats per compartment.

Along the way were water and wood stations, fuel to power the steam engine. The cars rode on strap iron nailed to green lumber, metal which frequently snapped and stuck up in the air. These "snakeheads" were a regular nuisance and workmen would walk the tracks nailing them back down. "How the railroad men of today would laugh at the thin straps 5/8 of an inch thick then spiked down," wrote Richard Mott, an early Toledo businessman and mayor in 1845-46.

While the train, which reached speeds as high as 20 miles per hour, was considered to be a local marvel, early travel certainly had its difficulties. An official of the railway boarded the northbound train at Palmyra, Michigan on an icy December day in 1841 intending to ride it to Adrian then back to his home in Toledo. He sat down, then changed his seat as there was a problem with the cushion.

*The Erie and Kalamazoo Railroad, with "Pleasure Car" in tow, chugs into the countryside.*

They had gone a half mile when a snakehead "came crashing through the floor of the car, passing diagonally through the seat I had left vacant, the end of the bar striking me in my neck under the chin and pushing me backward with such force as to break the panel work partition which divides the compartments of the car," he wrote. When the train came to a halt he found himself with his head and shoulders pushed through the partition and the snakehead grasped firmly in his hands. His heavy winter clothes prevented serious injury.

The offending snakeheads were spiked down and the train continued to Adrian and then turned around and left for Toledo at 7 p.m. The train worked its way slowly along the ice-covered track until it ran out of wood and water and "we picked up sticks in the woods and replenished the fire and with pails dipped up water from the ditches" and got under way.

About four miles past Sylvania they ran out of wood and water again, "so we left the locomotive and cars standing on the track and walked into the city, reaching there about 2:30 a.m. I was rather lame and sore from contact with the 'snakehead' but gratified that we were enjoying the 'modern improvement.'" Even though this "modern improvement" showed a profit in its first year, the railroad struggled financially after that and by 1842 was bankrupt, which was not surprising considering no one running the railroad had any experience.

"There was but little practical knowledge of the management of railroads, this being the first road in operation west of Utica, New York. How this road was got into operation and kept up, without money or credit, can never be fully explained and perhaps not entirely understood, even by the parties whose energy and pluck...carried it along through years of difficulty and embarrassment," wrote Richard Mott. However he credited the E. & K. R.R. "in settling the supremacy of Toledo as *the* business place at the west end of lake Erie over its several rival towns." In 1849 its road was turned over permanently to the Michigan Southern Railroad and the Erie & Kalamazoo Railroad, which never did make it to Kalamazoo, steamed into history.

Railroad tracks still pass through downtown Sylvania on the same route where once lay the strap iron and green lumber of the Erie & Kalamazoo. Where the tracks cross Monroe Street stands an historical marker telling that the first railroad west of the Alleghenies once clattered by there.

*The First Accident*

Railroad accidents were common in the early days and it wasn't long before the first railroad west of the Alleghenies had its first accident. "Distressing accident on the Erie and Kalamazoo Railroad," reported the January 10, 1838 edition of *The Toledo Blade*. A heavy rain had fallen the previous Saturday, washing out a railroad embankment and leaving the tracks high in the air. On Sunday morning the train came along on its usual run and the engineer saw the problem but was unable to stop in time.

The engine rode out on the unsupported rails which quickly gave way. In the plunge that followed, a fireman was impaled on an iron railing, killing him almost instantly. The engineer was crushed against the boiler "in which terrible situation he remained nearly fifteen minutes before he was extricated. He was dreadfully burnt and it is doubtful whether he will survive," the newspaper reported.

Two other firemen were either thrown or jumped from the train and were not injured and none of the passengers were hurt. The accident is believed to have occurred in an area where Wildwood Preserve Metropark is today. "This is the first accident which has occurred on our railroad," the article concluded, "and we trust that it may be the last."

# CHAPTER XII

THE UNDERGROUND RAILROAD

Carefully, quietly, they traveled north looking over their shoulders and carrying a luggage of fear. They came to that great river known as the Ohio and crossed into the state of the same name, people hunted and wanted for the crime of wanting to breathe free.

They were slaves breaking their literal and figurative Southern chains and headed for the one place they could be sure shackles would not be clamped on them again: Canada. Once these slaves reached Ohio, many virtually disappeared into a secretive system of hideouts and travel routes, frustrating pursuing slave catchers. The labyrinthine network that transported escaping slaves to their northern goal eventually came to be called the Underground Railroad. The places where the slaves stayed were "stations" and the people helping them "conductors."

Unlike other railroads, no records were kept, particularly when the Fugitive Slave Law of 1850 criminalized the helping of slaves with penalties of heavy fines, imprisonment, or both. Secrecy was essential and it was not unusual for the conductors and the slaves they were helping to avoid exchanging names. So most of the evidence collected over the years has been sketchy and anecdotal in form. Much of Ohio's history was collected by a young Ohio State professor, William Siebert. He became intrigued by reports from his students that their families had been involved in the Underground Railroad. Starting in 1891 he visited all the counties in Ohio, reading old newspaper accounts and interviewing these families, and even visiting southern Ontario and talking to former slaves who had escaped and had settled there.

Because of Ohio's geographical proximity to southern Canada and its number of religious and other abolitionist groups, Professor Siebert credited the state as being the busi-

© *Metroparks 1984*

*Artist's view of a fugitive slave family fleeing down a river with a "ghost tree," or sycamore, in the background. From the Underground Railroad display at the Edward and Prudence Lamb Heritage Center, Sidecut Metropark, Maumee. (Courtesy Toledo Area Metroparks).*

est in the North, with at least 23 routes. Several of the Underground Railroad lines passed through northwest Ohio. One ran on a trail through the present-day city of Bellefontaine, to Findlay, to Bowling Green and to Perrysburg [although not directly on this line, Fostoria had a home with a secret room that housed journeying slaves]. The other line came through Wapakoneta, to Lima, to Grand Rapids, then down the Maumee River. Both these routes would have passed through the Great Black Swamp.

Being the only major Lake Erie port between Cleveland and Toledo made Sandusky a major stop on the Underground Railroad. With a large number of conductors and over a dozen stations, Sandusky was given the code name "Hope" by railroad travelers. The dock at the foot of Columbus Street downtown was described by Harriet Beecher Stowe in her abolitionist novel *Uncle Tom's Cabin*.

While not cited by Siebert as a route, the banks of the Maumee River served as a path for some, as did the towpath of the Miami and Erie Canal which one could take from Cincinnati to the Maumee River near Defiance then down to Toledo.

Travel was done primarily at night while fleeing slaves were hidden during the day in secret rooms, lofts of barns, and in thick woods, to name a few. Another advantage of traveling at night was that the Big Dipper constellation in the northern sky provided a reliable beacon towards freedom. There was a song, *Follow the Drinking Gourd*, sung by escaping slaves that contained coded instructions as exemplified in the following stanza:

> *The river bank makes a very good road*
> *The dead trees show you the way*
> *Left foot, peg foot, traveling on*
> *Follow the drinking gourd*

The drinking gourd is the Big Dipper and the dead trees are sycamores that frequently line river banks and whose mottled, peeling bark frequently gives them the appearance of being dead. The river of the song was the Tennessee whose route went directly north into Kentucky although the instructions could have just as easily been applied to the Maumee River.

There were a number of area persons who were conductors on the Underground Railroad although history records only a few of their names. According to Professor Siebert, Edward Howard of Grand Rapids hid fleeing slaves in the woods near Grand Rapids before guiding them down the Maumee River to cross Lake Erie on boats. He credits him with being the first area white to do so, starting in the 1820's.

Edward Howard's son Dresden accompanied his father on some of his journeys. An aging Dresden Howard met with Siebert in the 1890's and recalled one such trip. His father was preparing to guide a group of fugitive slaves down the Maumee Valley and was wary of a man named Richardson who lived near Roche de Boeuf and made his living catching slaves.

"In order to avoid being surprised by this man it was necessary to keep a close lookout; and for greater safety the trip north from my father's was always performed at night," Howard recalled. "We had a whisper from an Indian friend that this [fugitive] party, which we had kept concealed in the thick, swampy forest near our cabin for some time, was being watched and would be ambushed on the way."

The night they left, Howard's father plotted an indirect route and posted a rear guard with instructions to shoot the horses of any pursuers. The Howard party had proceeded a few miles when the thunder of horse's hooves could be heard in the distance. A short time later "the sharp crack of a rifle echoed through the forest and the horse with a groan plunged to the ground," Howard said. "This checked the pursuing party and gave stimulus and speed to the feet of the fugitives. The slave catchers were now afraid to advance and retreated over the trail and the fugitives, though badly frightened, were permitted to continue their march to freedom unmolested."

For those slaves traveling to Michigan to cross the Detroit River into Canada, Sylvania was a stop on the Underground Railroad with at least three stations. Maumee and Perrysburg had safe houses as well and slaves were often hidden in buildings in downtown Toledo waiting for a ship to take them across Lake Erie

Those who took the time and risk to help escaping slaves pass safely through on the Underground Railroad were heroic. It would have been just as easy to turn their back, especially in light of the criminal penalties helping slaves could bring.

Perhaps the most heroic were the slaves themselves who, despite tremendous risk, undertook journeys of great danger, fear their constant companion. They traveled with little more than the clothes on their backs knowing that every snap of a twig or rustle of trees could mean a slave catcher was upon them. And once in Canada they were far from family and loved ones in a climate they had never before experienced, strangers in a strange land. It is believed upwards of 75,000 slaves had made the journey by the start of the Civil War, a steep price for freedom.

*This historic home on South Main Street in Sylvania is believed to have been a station on the Underground Railroad. The house dates back to at least 1832.*

# CHAPTER XIII

LAURA HAVILAND, ABOLITIONIST

It was an apprehensive trio that rode the Erie and Kalamazoo Railroad toward Toledo one afternoon in 1846. On the train was an Adrian abolitionist named Laura Haviland, her 17-year-old son Daniel, and a friend of theirs, a black man named James Martin. Their destination was the old Toledo House hotel on Summit Street.

There they would investigate their suspicions that slave catchers were in town conducting an elaborate ruse to lure an escaped slave living on Laura Haviland's land to Toledo for capture. The escaped slave's name was Elsie Hamilton, who had fled the South with her husband Willis. He was a freed slave working in Tennessee to buy her freedom when he heard of her owner's plan to sell her. They fled to Canada but, finding little work, came to the Adrian area where anti-slavery Quakers like Laura Haviland provided refuge and land to farm.

Once established in Michigan, Willis and Elsie Hamilton sent a letter to Willis' former owner, a Baptist preacher who had turned against slavery and freed Willis along with the rest of his slaves. The Hamiltons were hoping the preacher could help locate two of their children still enslaved somewhere in the South. The danger in such a communication was that it would reveal their whereabouts.

Sure enough, the letter fell into the hands of Elsie's former owner who came North with his son and son-in-law in the role as slave catchers. Arriving in Toledo they sent a bogus letter to the Hamiltons, writing as if the letter came from the preacher himself and saying he was in Toledo on business and had become very ill and wished to see Willis and Elsie at the hotel. Laura Haviland suspected a ruse and told Willis and Elsie Hamilton not to respond, that she would go to Toledo to investigate. Laura Haviland was no ordinary woman.

Born in 1809, Haviland grew up in upper New York state. There she had her first encounter with a black man, a kindly, elderly gentleman who hawked merchandise in the streets of her village. When a gang of local boys hurled mud at the man and yelled racial epithets, the seeds of racial justice were planted in her mind. And when she read a book that detailed the horrible conditions on slave ships and on Southern planta- tions, these seeds became abolitionist roots.

In the late 1820's she moved with her husband to the Raisin River Valley in the Adrian, Michigan area. There a number of New York state Quakers had established farms and there Laura Haviland helped found the first anti-slavery society in Michi- gan. In 1837 she and her brother established the Raisin Insti- tute, a school that admitted blacks, which was almost unheard of at the time. In 1845 an outbreak of disease had taken the lives of her husband, parents, one of her children, and had nearly killed her. A year later found her on a train making a strange journey to Toledo.

She arrived in town with her traveling companions and went to the Toledo House to inquire about this allegedly ill Baptist preacher. What unfolded there was an almost comical cloak and dagger performance involving an earnest and caring doc- tor, the terribly ill Baptist preacher whose face was covered with damp cloths, and the preacher's deeply concerned son.

To make a long story short, the trio from the South went to great play-acting lengths to convince Laura Haviland that the "ill" man laying in his room was the dying Baptist preacher wanting to see his former slave Willis and his wife Elsie. As it turned out the role of the ill preacher was played by one of the slave catchers, the part of the concerned son by the other catcher, with Elsie's former owner himself featured as the doc- tor. This theater of the absurd dragged on half the night. The whole charade was put on because the slave catchers were afraid to go into abolitionist country to snatch their intended victim.

At one point during this bizarre night Haviland's black friend, James Martin, was briefly kidnapped by the slave catchers but he lied his way out of it by agreeing to cooperate for money. Laura Haviland, too, gave the illusion of cooperating, pretending to believe their ridiculous production and telling the three she would return to Adrian the next morning and advise Willis and Elsie Hamilton it was safe to come to Toledo.

The next morning she reboarded the train for Adrian with her son and James Martin. However the slave catchers got on the train as well, apparently not believing any cooperation would really be forthcoming. The slave catcher who had played the ill preacher, followed Laura Haviland about the train from one coach to another until finally some friends of hers threw a protective cordon around her. Then the train's conductor, in a loud voice, vouched for the personal safety of all

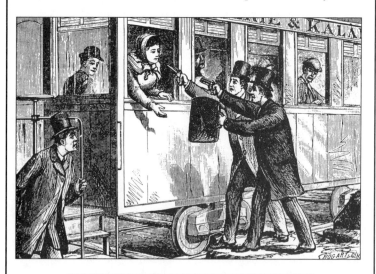

*Laura Haviland is confronted by the slave catch-*

*ers on the Erie and Kalamazoo Railroad near*

*Sylvania.*

his passengers, and the slave catchers realized they were not going to get what they came all the way from Tennessee for. Now they were frustrated and angry.

Near Sylvania the train stopped for some track maintenance and the slave catchers got off. First they made threats to James Martin and to Laura's son, then drew their pistols. They then pointed their guns directly at Laura's face, and shook a traveling bag at her, saying they had more guns inside. "And we know how to use them," shouted Elsie's former owner. "We shall stay about here three weeks and we will have that property you have in your possession yet, you damned nigger stealer. We understand ourselves. We know what we are about!"

She stared at them and replied calmly, "Man, I fear neither your weapons nor your threats, they are powerless. You are not at home; you are not in Tennessee. And as for your property, I have none of it about me or on my premises. We also understand what we are about; we also understand, not only ourselves, but you."

The slave catchers were now trembling with rage, still pointing their guns. By now they were attracting a lot of attention and the conductor bellowed, "What are you doing here you villainous scoundrels? We'll have you arrested in five minutes!" At this point the slave catchers went running for the woods, "and the last we saw of these tall and valiant representatives of the land of chivalry were their heels fast receding in the thicket."

The train went on to Adrian, the passengers all abuzz. Word of the incident raced about Sylvania and upwards of 40 men with iron bars assembled at the Sylvania depot ready to tear up the tracks if the train returned with the slave catchers and their intended victim. The catchers however, returned South empty handed, but Elsie's former owner did send abusive and threatening letters to Haviland, letters she responded to in kind. And at one point a reward was placed on her head in parts of the South.

Laura Haviland continued her anti-slavery work through the Civil War and worked to help freed blacks after it. In later years she campaigned for prison reform and better conditions for the poor, worked for temperance causes, established a home for wayward girls, and survived a fall that fractured her skull. She died in 1898 after a series of strokes. And in 1909 the city of Adrian honored her life and work by erecting a statue of her in front of City Hall.

*This statue of Laura Haviland stands in front*

*of City Hall in Adrian, Michigan.*

# CHAPTER XIV

THE LAST CHIPPEWA

During the 19th century transition that changed northwest Ohio from a Native domain to one dominated by Europeans, one of those Natives remained, a Chippewa named Victoria Cadaract. Like so many persons and events of history, a bit of mystery shrouds her story.

She reported childhood memories of Indians and soldiers on the march to clash at Fort Meigs in 1813 which would have made her well over 100 years old when she died in 1915. But census records indicate she was born in 1828 and gave birth in 1864 and 1866 which would have been during normal child bearing years. If she was in fact born in 1828 she easily could have had childhood memories of soldiers coming to march Indians toward western exile which they did in the 1830's and early 1840's.

She was born in Ohio as were both her parents. Her grandfather was believed to have been chief of a Chippewa tribe that at one time owned land around the mouth of the Maumee River. Her father died when she was young and her mother was remarried to Francis Navarre, older brother of Toledo pioneer Peter Navarre.

Victoria Cadaract herself married a half French man who died relatively young, leaving her a widow for the bulk of her life. She lived in a cabin on a large farm owned by the Taylor family near Curtice in Ottawa County where the Chippewa Golf Club is now. She grew her own vegetables and regularly walked the two miles into town to buy goods she needed, even when beyond the age of eighty and blind in one eye.

She was proud and did not accept charity although people tried to help. A local newspaper reported in December, 1898, "the people of Curticeville held a box social at the church Wednesday night for the benefit of Mrs. Cadaract, an old Indian woman."

In 1914 she was invited to attend the Independence Day dedication of the Navarre Monument in Navarre Park in East Toledo but didn't show. A *Toledo Daily Blade* reporter went to investigate and she told him she had not done her washing and "could not think of going out unless her wearing apparel was in order." She also admitted she was tired and was having difficulty getting around

The following March she was found unconscious on the floor

*Victoria Cadaract stands in front of her cabin in this undated photo. (Photo courtesy of the Ottawa County Historical Society).*

of her cabin with a broken hip. She died of pneumonia in the Ottawa County Infirmary a couple of weeks later. She was buried in an unmarked grave in Crane Creek Cemetery near Curtice in a plot she had she had purchased in 1884 for two dollars.

So it seemed her story would end there, just another un-marked and forgotten grave in a small, rural cemetery. But in 1984 the Ottawa County Historical Society erected a marker in the cemetery acknowledging her burial there, along with that of a five-year-old Native girl named Mary Sword who died in 1879. Crane Creek Cemetery is one of only a small num-ber known Native-American burial sites in northwest Ohio.

# CHAPTER XV

GHOST TOWNS OF THE MAUMEE

Most of the names were little more than a speculator's fancy on an early Maumee Valley map. Towns such as Marengo, East Marengo, Lucas City, Orleans of the North, Austerlitz and Manhattan passed from dreams to dust in a few years during the 1820's and 1830's. Only Manhattan actually had any bricks and mortar to speak of before becoming part of the new city of Toledo. Marengo died a rapid death despite its founder's prediction that "at no distant day Marengo will be the largest town in Western Ohio."

Two river towns that did take root and flourish for a time were Miltonville and Providence. There, settlers from the increasingly crowded eastern seaboard could afford a lot, build a cabin, and begin what they hoped would be a long life story. Both towns were platted in 1835 and both got off to good starts. But both would struggle for various reasons and die, ghost towns of the Maumee.

Providence, located directly across the river from present-day Grand Rapids, was the much more prosperous of the two. It was laid out by a colorful French Canadian named Peter Manor, an Americanized version of his given name of Pierre Menard. He was a fur trader and one of the earliest white settlers of the Maumee Valley, coming to what is now the city of Maumee in 1816. He made friends with the Ottawa tribe headed by Chief Tontogany who adopted him as a son and gave him the Indian name of Yellow Hair. Peter Manor built a sawmill in 1822, a schoolhouse in 1828, and a gristmill around 1835. One of the first things Manor did in his new town of Providence was open a tavern, and taverns would play a role in the town's history.

By 1840 Providence was thriving, with five hotels, four general stores and warehouses on the Maumee River. The town was also swelling with canal workers as the Miami and Erie Canal and Lock #44 (also once called Lock #9) were being dug literally through the center of town. Many of the canal workers shared the same off duty recreational pursuits, drinking and fighting. And some nights free-for-all brawls tumbled through the streets of Providence and word spread that it was no place for decent folk to live.

In 1843 the canal opened and the economy in Providence boomed. Lock #44 in town became an overnight stop for many canal travelers despite its reputation for lawlessness. In 1845 St. Patrick's Roman Catholic Church opened to serve the large Irish population that had settled there, many who had come to work on the canal. In 1846 Isaac Ludwig built a large, three-story mill on the site of Peter Manor's mill and things were looking good for Providence.

However in 1846 a major fire swept through the central business district and many of the buildings were never rebuilt. In 1854 some canal boat passengers disembarked and brought the cholera epidemic that was sweeping through the Midwest. The dreaded disease cut like a scythe through the town and people fled, some never to return. St. Patrick's Cemetery became a weeping ground as scores of Providence residents were laid to rest, their graves overlooking the canal that many of them labored to dig.

Some of the 1854 gravestones there are still legible. In spring of that year a grieving Michael Connolly buried his 22-year-old wife Ann and on her marker was chiseled a warning:

> Shed not for her the bitter tear
> Nor give the heart to vain regret
> Tis but the casket that lies here
> The germ that filled it sparkles yet

The cholera epidemic ran its course but a different sort of death was taking place. The canals, which were supposed to guarantee decades of economic prosperity, were already being replaced by the railroad. Providence slowly drifted into history until removed from county records in 1928.

*Part of the ghost town of Providence lives*

*on in the Isaac Ludwig Mill, built in 1846,*

*and now operated by Toledo Area*

*Metroparks.*

Today the Toledo Area Metroparks not only preserves the town's name in Providence Metropark but has restored and operates the Isaac Ludwig Mill, a section of the canal, and the lock itself, complete with a working canal boat. And St. Patrick's Church still stands on US 24, a marker on its lawn telling of the town's history. While Providence certainly meets the working definition of a ghost town, images of its past will long remain.

The same cannot be said for Miltonville, a town hard on the Maumee River, and across and a mile or so upriver from present-day Waterville. It was platted in 1835 in a low area along the river where a sizable cabin and store had been built a couple of years earlier. That year a man named Joel Foote bought the cabin and remodeled it into The Foote Hotel. This was followed by another hotel, The Uncle Guy House, built by a character well known to early Wood County history, "Uncle" Guy Nearing.

This was followed by a post office in 1837, the establishment of a rope ferry for purposes of crossing the river, and the construction of a sawmill and dam about a half mile downriver by Guy Nearing. After that the town sort of faded away for unclear reasons.

Like Providence, the town was struck by cholera and its low location on the river probably led to a few floods which could have contributed to its demise. One theory that has been offered is that Miltonville was established where it was only because it was thought the canal would come through on that side of the Maumee River. When the canal went through on the opposite side, momentum for sustaining a town waned.

In 1859 the Miltonville post office was transferred to nearby Haskins when the railroad was completed there. The loss of the post office is a death knell for any town. And an 1886 Wood County atlas indicates just six structures and no businesses in the town. None of those structures stand today.

Two of Miltonville's original streets remain, Front Street, now State Route 65 (River Rd.), and Lucas Street, now Ovitt Road. There's a gravel parking lot for fisherman about where the center of town once was with an historical marker telling of Miltonville's past. And on the slope of a nearby ravine are the remnants of the town's cemetery. There a handful of crumbling tombstones slant under the shade of an aging oak tree. Their inscriptions largely erased by time, they reveal no further secrets about the ghost town of Miltonville.

The dreams of the founders of Miltonville of a riverside town lasted only a few decades. The only trace of the town today is a small, aging cemetery.

# CHAPTER XVI

## THE GREAT WHIG GATHERING OF 1840

It was the tenth day of June, 1840 and a fleet like nothing seen before fell into line on the Maumee River. Steamers from the major Lake Erie ports, their decks thick with humanity, left downtown Toledo and sailed up the Maumee River. With colorful banners flapping in the breeze, bands playing, and cannons firing, people on the shore shouted and waved as they passed by. Their destination was Perrysburg and the grounds of Fort Meigs for the great Whig gathering of 1840.

Waiting there were thousands of fellow Whigs from at least seven states, there to acclaim their candidate for president, former general William Henry Harrison of Ohio. As the day wore on thousands more arrived in decorated wagons and carriages in parade formation, one procession having more than 500 wagons. Included in the gathering that swelled the roads leading to northwest Ohio were entire military companies from several states.

Thousands of tents popped up around the grounds of the old fort and revelers dipped from hundreds of barrels of hard cider. An East Coast paper months earlier had sneered that Harrison might be more comfortable spending the rest of his days in a log cabin with an unlimited supply of hard cider and the Whigs had seized on this, making hard cider and log cabins campaign themes.

Around 6 p.m. a steamer from Sandusky carrying the old general himself came downriver and people clung from every treetop, roof, and ships rigging to see their hero. Cannons fired in salute as Harrison made his way to the fort. After reviewing the troops there and fatigued from a long day, he retired to the mansion of a Perrysburg judge.

But the crowd was just getting warmed up. As the sun began to set, over 20,000 were on the fort's grounds, singing songs, listening to bands and speeches, and dipping their ladles deep into the barrels of hard cider which was "free as water." Few were in a mood to sleep and at midnight trumpets sounded and guns and cannons lit the sky as a mock attack on the fort was acted out. A Detroit newspaper reported, "the rushing of the soldiery as they changed position to repel the attacks of the assailants–the burnished musket as it cast back reflections of moonbeams–presented a spectacle really magnificent..."

Despite the long night of celebration a Buffalo paper reported that "not a single drunken or quarrelsome man could be seen" and the dawn was greeted with a 100 gun salute. In the morning thousands of local and area residents began arriving and by 10 a.m. the crowd had swelled to over 25,000, a remarkable number considering the limited travel opportunities available in 1840.

Soon Harrison appeared at the fort and ascended the podium to tumultuous cheers that echoed down the Maumee Valley. While waiting for the din to die down he likely reflected on his previous triumphs there: successfully withstanding the two sieges of Fort Meigs as commander in 1813 and serving as Anthony Wayne's aide during the Battle of Fallen Timbers across the river in 1794.

Harrison gave a 90 minute speech under a burning sun during some of which he talked of the pressures and loneliness of command. "I could point from where I now stand to places where I felt this anxiety pressing heavily upon me as I thought of the fearful consequences of a mistake on my part or the want of judgment on the part of others. I knew there were wives–mothers who had clothed their sons for battle; and I knew that these expecting wives and mothers were looking for the safe return of their husbands and sons...Feeling my responsibility I personally supervised and directed the arrangement of the army under my command. I trusted no other Colonel or officer."

Harrison's speech was followed by a number of others and interspersed with the singing of political songs and the meeting lasted until darkness before breaking up. Thus ended what was considered at the time to be one of the more remarkable political conventions ever held in the United States and to this day probably one of the more remarkable ones in the history of Ohio.

The momentum of those two days in June, 1840 carried over and in November Harrison carried 19 of 26 states to become the first president from the Buckeye State. However his love of long speeches would prove to be his undoing. On March 4, 1841, Inauguration Day, he gave a nearly two hour speech on a raw and windy day wearing no hat or coat. By the end of the month a cold had developed into pneumonia and on April 4th, he died. The first president from Ohio also became the first to die in office.

*William Henry Harrison, Anthony Wayne's aide in 1794 and commander of Fort Meigs in 1813, returned to the fort to preside at the great Whig gathering of 1840.*

# CHAPTER XVII

SNAPSHOTS

*1. The Keeper's House*

Only 23 stars were emblazoned on the United States' flag when the foundation for this old stone house was laid in 1821. Finished the following year, it was home to Benajah and Rachel Wolcott, first keepers of the Marblehead light.

Benajah Wolcott was the first permanent settler in what became Ottawa County, a pioneer in the truest sense. A veteran of the American Revolution, he first came to Ohio in 1806 as part of the Fire Lands Survey Team. The firelands was a half million acre tract of Ohio land set aside for Connecticut settlers whose lands had been burned during the Revolution. He returned in 1809 and built a log cabin on the Marblehead peninsula near where the stone house is now. Years of work and hardship followed, including two years of forced relocation during the War of 1812, during which his first wife died.

He returned to the peninsula in 1814, a widower with three children. Legend has it that his was the only cabin not burned by Indians during the war due to his friendship with an area Wynadot chief. In 1821 he became first keeper of the Marblehead Lighthouse and in 1822, now married to Rachel, he moved into his fine stone house which had to be quite a step up from the frontier log cabins of the day. He lived ten more years before dying in a cholera epidemic in 1832. Rachel Wolcott then took over his duties, the first female lighthouse keeper on the Great Lakes, a position in which she served until 1854. Both are buried in a nearby family cemetery.

The house, with its 28-inch thick limestone walls and hand hewn chestnut and walnut beams, remains as a rare intact example of an early American architectural style known as a hall and parlor house. Over the years it served as residence and at one point a restaurant. The 1980's found it in deteriorating condition and very much in need of repair. It was acquired in 1989 by the Ottawa County Historical Society and renovations restoring it to its period condition are continuing. It is now open for summertime tours.

The Keeper's House is the oldest residence in Ottawa County and quite possibly in all of northwest Ohio. Its existence dates back to the earliest days of white settlement in the area.

*This stone house on Bayshore Road on the Marblehead Peninsula was built in 1822 and was home to the first keepers of the Marblehead Light, Benajah and Rachel Wolcott. Following the death of her husband, Rachel became the first female keeper on the Great Lakes.*

*2. Hessville, Ohio*

The following comes from a hand written, undated manuscript titled *Hessville, The Heart of the Black Swamp*. It was found in the belongings of a deceased resident of a Toledo nursing home in the 1970's and reprinted in the Fall, 1977, edition of the *Northwest Ohio Quarterly*. Only the name of the writer, C. H. Opperman, is known. Hessville, a village that sprung up circa 1837 in Sandusky County along the Maumee and Western Reserve Road (now US 20), still exists today. As the writer makes reference to the state of Ohio building the road "about one Hundred years ago," the manuscript probably was written in the 1920 to 1940 time frame.

C. H. Opperman described the early and generally futile efforts to create a road out of the Black Swamp, a road that in its early days was considered to be the worst road in America. Workers toiled 12 hours a day cutting down and burning the great trees that stood in the way, then graded the ground. "A Bank of muck and mud twenty feet wide and about Three feet high was build mostly by Ox Power...The grade was finished it was called a road but in reality it was only a bank of mud."

Westward travelers took it anyway, Opperman explained, thinking they could save time over the longer, but dryer southern route of Tiffin to Findlay to Fort Wayne. "Nearly all of Them Who Took the Swamp route regretted Their unwise decision, for many of Them had Ox teams to draw–Their high-wheeled covered wagons. Often The Oxen would sink to Their bellys and The wheels to The hubbs and in many cases made only a mile or two of progress in a day. When night came They were compelled to build camp fires and sleep in Their wagons..."

Over time taverns were built along the road and travelers for the most part stayed in them. The road was so bad the state finally paved it [1838-39] with "twelve inches of hand broken stone," according to Opperman. "As i now remember when a little boy i could see an unbroken line of Covered wagons going over This Pike."

Toll gates were erected every eight miles with a charge of 25 cents, and covered bridges, including one in Hessville, were built over the rivers and creeks, providing shelter for travelers caught in a rainstorm, according to Opperman. "They allso furnished much pleasure to The children who lived near Them as we would climb up on The sides on The Crosstimbers and around on the joists overhead. In many cases Horses were frightened by our actions as They were driven Through."

Hessville went through a bit of an identity crisis before its current name was settled on, Opperman explained. It was originally called Cash Town after a Mr. Cash who had established a general store. Then a Mr. Hess built a store on the opposite side of the road and that side was known as Hess Town. Eventually Mr. Cash moved away and both sides were called Hess Town even though the post office was called The Black Swamp Office. It wasn't until the 1870's that the name Hessville was settled on.

Times were good in the early days of Hessville, according

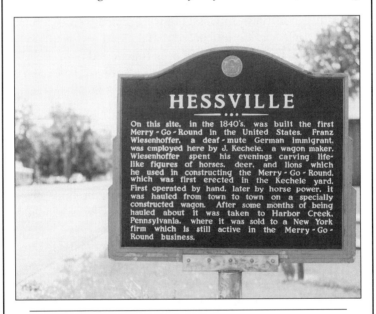

*Thousands of westward-bound settlers and their covered wagons once streamed through Hessville on the Maumee and Western Reserve Road. And the first merry-go-round in the United States was built in there in the 1840's.*

to Opperman. The town had "two General Stores. Three Taverns, Three Salloons, two Blacksmith shops, Two Waggon Shops, two Copper shops, a basket shop, a tannery, a Pottash still or ashers as it was called, a Harness and Collar shop, a Monument shop, a sorgum Mill, [and] two shoe and Boot shops..."

There also was a gristmill powered by both water and steam. "To This Mill a distillery was added where Corn, Rhy & Potato Whiskey was made...whiskey of one hundred proof was sold from That place for 15 cts a Gallon or 2 Gallons for 25 cts. This industry made a market for Corn and by That time The Swamp had developed into a Corn County. My Father and I hauled many loads of it to That distillery at eighteen cents per bushel. Many cattle and hogs were fattened on The by product from the still."

But the good times in Hessville were short lived. A 1909 history of Sandusky County noted that the mill and distillery were gone and the post office had been transferred to a nearby town, the latter a clear indication that the growth days were over. The history also made the observation, "the village has not increased in population of late years to any appreciable extent," a polite way of saying Hessville was fading.

Hessville's early growth was no doubt due to the "unbroken line of covered wagons" Opperman witnessed as a boy. Once the pioneers were no longer coming through and patronizing the blacksmiths, general stores and wagon shops etc., most of the businesses dried up. Today Hessville is a small village with little commerce.

But Hessville has an enduring claim to fame not referred to by Mr. Opperman. One of the immigrants who came to Hessville was a German man named Franz Wiesenhofer who was unable to hear or speak. Locked in a world of silence he spent his evenings carving life-like animals which were used to build the first merry-go-round ever constructed in the United States. The merry-go-round, built by a Hessville wagon maker, delighted the children of Hessville and the area before being sold. Perhaps one of those children was a boy named C. H. Opperman.

### 3. The Oak Tree

The year was 1836 and in a frontier cabin in Henry County a baby girl named Martha Edwards Showman was born, the first white child born in Washington Township. To celebrate the occasion, local Ottawa Indians planted an oak tree on a high bank of the Maumee River.

In the next two years there were two major movements of Ottawa Indians west beyond the Mississippi River. The little girl probably never got to know those who planted the tree in her name.

The tree, however, has thrived. Now in its third century, it has grown tall and full, a mighty oak soaring high above the Maumee River. Its existence harkens to a brief period in time when Native-Americans and settlers lived peacefully together.

*This oak tree on US 24 in Henry County was planted in 1836 by Ottawa Indians in honor of the first white child born in Washington Township.*

### 4. Fulton County Indian Photo

The photo below hangs in a quiet room at the Fulton County Historical Museum in Wauseon. That one day in time, 11 Native-Americans and one white man posed for a photo is apparent. The names of eight of the Natives and of the white man are written on the photo itself. Nothing else is known about it.

Where or when the photo was taken or what tribes are represented is a mystery. From whom or when the museum acquired the photo is also unknown. It's a remarkable photo that gives an actual peek into the past that normally is illustrated only with words and artistic images. Unfortunately, it leaves many questions unanswered, ones that may never be answered. Any one with any further knowledge or information about the photo can contact the Fulton County Historical Society, 229 Monroe St., Wauseon, OH 43567.

*This photo of 11 Native-Americans and one white man hangs in the Fulton County Museum, Wauseon. The names as written from left to right are: Back Row: Big Snake, Balice, White Eagle, Charles La Clair, Yellow Bull. Front Row: Unnamed, White Swan, Unnamed, Standing Buffalo, Unnamed, Big Smoke. On Floor: Black Bear. (Photo courtesy of Fulton County Historical Society, Wauseon.)*

## 5. The Mull Covered Bridge

Over 10,000 covered bridges were built in the United States between 1805 and the early 20th century and over 90% of those bridges have passed into history. One that remains is the Mull Covered Bridge in Sandusky County.

It was built by Henry Mull and his family in 1851 to provide a way over Wolf Creek and access to his mill. Weather was the principle reason bridges were covered. The bridge decks lasted longer being protected from the elements. In addition, the cover kept a layer of ice from building up in the winter which would make for a treacherous crossing for a wagon and team.

For over 100 years vehicles powered by horses, and later, horsepower, rumbled over it before it was closed in 1962. It has since been listed on the National Register of Historic Places, a pioneer in its own right.

*This covered bridge over Wolf Creek in Sandusky County was built in 1851 and carried traffic for over 100 years before being closed in 1962.*

# ABOUT THE AUTHOR

Jim Mollenkopf is a Toledo, Ohio, free-lance writer and author who enjoys local history. A former social worker then newspaper reporter, he wrote and published *Lake Erie Sojourn: an autumn tour of the parks, public places, and history of the lake erie shore* in 1998 and *The Great Black Swamp: historical tales of 19th century northwest Ohio* in 1999.

# REFERENCES

Beers, J.H. *Commemorative Historical and Biographical Record of Wood County, Ohio.* Chicago: J.H. Beers, 1897.

Bennett, John. *Blue Jacket: War Chief of the Shawnees.* Chillicothe: Ross County Historical Society Press, 1943.

Bourne, Alexander. "The Siege of Fort Meigs Year 1813." *Northwest Ohio Quarterly,* 17 & 18 (Oct. 1945 & Jan. 1946) 139, 39.

Buell, John. *The Diary of John Hutchinson Buell.* Richard C. Knopf (ed.). Columbus: The Anthony Wayne Parkway Board, 1957.

Buchman, Randall. *The Confluence.* Defiance: The Defiance College Press, 1994.

Carter, Harvey L. *The Life and Times of Little Turtle.* Chicago: University of Illinois Press, 1987.

Cunningham, J.W. "All Aboard for Miltonville!" *Northwest Ohio Quarterly,* 22 (Fall, 1950) 209.

Dwarko, Daniel A. *The Settler in The Maumee Valley: Henry, Lucas, and Wood Counties Ohio, 1830-1860,* Thesis No. 671 (Ph.D.) Bowling Green State University, 1981.

Evers, Charles W. *The Pioneer Scrap-Book.* Bowling Green: The Democrat, 1910.

Fabin, W.W. "Indians of the Tri-State Area, The Potawatomis, The Removal." *Northwest Ohio Quarterly,* 40 (Summer, 1968) 68.

Gillespie, Ray. *Indians Along the Maumee River.* Toledo: Up and Running Inc., 1994.

Gindy, Gaye E. *Next Stop Sylvania, Ohio.* Sylvania: Sylvania Historical Village Inc. 1998.

Glaab, Charles N. and Morgan, Barclay J. *Toledo: Gateway to the Great Lakes.* Tulsa: Continental Heritage Press, 1982.

Gunckel, John. *The Early History of the Maumee Valley.* Toledo: Hadley Printing, 1902.

Gunderson, Robert G. "The Fort Meigs Whig Celebration of 1840." *Northwest Ohio Quarterly,* 21 ( Spring, 1949) 69.

Gunderson, Robert G. *The Log-Cabin Campaign.* Lexington: University of Kentucky Press, 1957.

Harvey, Henry. *History of the Shawnee Indians.* Cincinnati: Ephraim Morgan & Sons, 1855.

Haviland, Laura S. *A Woman's Life Work.* Chicago: Publishing Association of Friends, 1889.

Hosmer, Hezekiah L. & Harris W.H. *Early History of the Maumee Valley.* Toledo: Hosmer and Harris, 1858.

Howe, Henry. *Historical Collections of Ohio* (V. 1 & 2). Cincinnati: C. J. Krebiel & Co., 1888.

Howard, Dresden. "The Last Gathering Under the Old Council Elm. Robert F. Bauman (ed.) *Northwest Ohio Quarterly,* 29 (Summer, 1957) 144.

Huffman, June *The Providence Record, 1981.* Defiance: The Hubbard Printing Company, 1982.

Kaatz. Martin R. *The Settlement of the Black Swamp of Northwestern Ohio.* Thesis (Ph.D.) University of Michigan, 1952.

Keller, Kathryn M. "Sylvania Chronicle: The E & K: First Railroad West of the Alleghenies." *Northwest Ohio Quarterly,* 46 (Fall, 1974) 136.

Keller, Kathryn M. "Sylvania Chronicle: Stations Along the Underground Railroad." *Northwest Ohio Quarterly,* 47 (Winter 1974-75) 30.

Knapp, Horace S. *History of the Maumee Valley.* Toledo: Blade Mammoth Printing, 1872.

Landon, Fred. "Over Lake Erie to Freedom." *Northwest Ohio Quarterly,* 17 (Oct. 1945) 132.

Meek, Basil. *Twentieth Century History of Sandusky County, Ohio.* Chicago: Richmond-Arnold Publishing, 1909.

Michaels, Larry R. *East Side Story.* Toledo: Bihl House Publishing, 1993.

# References (continued)

Miller, Lillian M. "Aunt Laura: The Story of Laura Haviland." *Northwest Ohio Quarterly,* 24 (Fall, 1952) 199.

Repp, Philip. *Words and Images: Land Within the Maumee.* Muncie: Minnetrista Cultural Center, 1990.

Scribner, Harvey. *Memoirs of Lucas County and the City of Toledo.* Madison, WI: Western Historical Association, 1910.

Siebert, Wilbur H. *The Mysteries of Ohio's Underground Railroads.* Columbus: Long College Book Company, 1951.

Siebert, Wilbur H. *The Underground Railroad in Ohio.* Ohio Archeological and Historical Publications, 4 1895.

Simonis, Louis A. *Maumee River, 1835.* Defiance: Defiance County Historical Society, 1979.

Smith, Dwight L. *Wayne's Peace with the Indians of the Old Northwest.* Public Library of Fort Wayne, 1955?

Spears, John R. *Anthony Wayne: Sometimes Called "Mad Anthony."* New York: D. Appleton and Company, 1903.

Sword, Wiley. *President Washington's Indian War.* Norman: University of Oklahoma Press, 1985.

Tracy, J.R. *"Reminiscent." Addresses, Memorials, and Sketches.* Toledo: The Maumee Valley Pioneer Association, 1900.

Wilhelm, Peter. *Draining the Black Swamp: Henry and Wood Counties.* Thesis No. 4295 (M.A.) Bowling Green State University, 1983.

Wendler, Marilyn V. "Anti-Slavery Sentiment and the Underground Railroad in the Lower Maumee Valley." *Northwest Ohio Quarterly,* 52 (Spring, 1980) 193.

_____*A Bicentennial History of Hillsdale County Michigan* V 1. Hillsdale: Hillsdale County Historical Society and the Hillsdale County Bicentennial Commission, 1976.

_____*An Atlas of Wood County Ohio.* Bowling Green: The Maumee Valley Map Company, ND.

_____*Anthony Wayne: A Name in Arms.* Richard C. Knopf

(ed.). Pittsburgh: University of Pittsburgh Press, 1960.

_____ *Atlas of Great Lakes Indian History.* Helen Hornbeck Tanner (ed.). Norman: University of Oklahoma Press, 1987.

_____*From Greene Ville to Fallen Timbers.* Dwight L. Smith (ed.). Indiana Historical Society, 1952.

_____*History of Sandusky County, Ohio.* Cleveland: H.Z. Williams & Bro., 1882.

_____*History of the City of Toledo and Lucas County, Ohio.* Clark Waggoner (ed.) New York: Munsell and Co., 1888.

_____*A Standard History of Williams County, Ohio.* V. 1. Charles A. Bowersox (ed.). New York: The Lewis Publishing Company, 1920.

*Other Sources*

"Distressing Accident on the Erie and Kalamazoo." *The Toledo Blade,* January 10, 1838

"Indian Woman of 1812 is Failing." *Toledo Daily Blade,* July 10, 1914.

"Peter Navarre: Scout, Woodsman, Patriot." *Toledo Daily Blade,* ?? ?? 1905.

Letters of Samuel Skinner. From a descendant.

The Dresden Howard Papers. Fulton County Historical Society, Wauseon.

Papers of Noah Prowant 1941-1962. Center for Archival Collections, Bowling Green State University.

Fallen Timbers Battlefield www.heidleberg.edu/fallentimbers

The Underground Railroad in Erie County, Ohio. www.buckeyenorth.com/underground